Trout Eyes

Trout Eyes

True Tales of Adventure, Travel, and Fly Fishing

WILLIAM G. TAPPLY

Skyhorse Publishing

www.skyhorsepublishing.com

10 9 8 7 6 5 4 3 2 1

Library of Congress Cataloging-in-Publication-Data
    Tapply, William G.
    Trout eyes / by William G. Tapply.
        p.   cm.
    ISBN-13: 978-1-60239-048-5 (hardcover : alk. paper)
    ISBN-10: 1-60239-048-7 (hardcover : alk. paper)
    1. Trout fishing—Anecdotes.   2. Fly fishing—Anecdotes.
  I. Title.

SH687.T277   2007
799.12'4—dc22
                                                          2006039598

Printed in the United States of America

TABLE OF CONTENTS

Foreword

Fly-fishing is a full-time occupation. Or preoccupation. Increasingly, I find that when I'm not on the water, I'm thinking about being on the water, or about the water itself, what's in it and what's floating on it and how pure it is, or about the fish that might be living in it and how I might catch them. I talk with my friends—and with strangers, too—about rivers and fish and flies and rods and reels. I daydream about brooks and rivers, ponds and lakes and oceans. I read fly-fishing magazines and books and watch cable television shows about fly fishing. I go to club meetings and shows. I haunt tackle shops.

Having fly fishing on the brain is almost as good as doing it. Actually, sometimes it's better. It hardly ever rains on my daydreams, and I rarely get skunked.

The musings in this book are the product of the past several years of my whimsical and undisciplined fly-fishing fantasies and fancies, as I remember the places I've been, the people I've met, the fish I've caught, and the fish I've failed to catch. These stories address the situations that make me happy, and angry, and sad, and philosophical, and frustrated.

Mostly happy.

Here there are stories about waters that have meant something to me—small places like Porcupine Brook, big places like the Atlantic Ocean, famous places like the Bighorn River, faraway places like Patagonia. There are stories about fish—particular fish like a tarpon I once met and a permit who met me halfway—and species of fish that especially interest me, like largemouth bass and striped bass and, of course, trout.

I write about casting and strategies, flies and bugs, equipment and rigs, and even how to catch fish, but I urge you not to take me too seriously on any of these subjects.

Here there are stories about people and stories inspired by people. They are all real people, although some, like my father and virtually all of his friends, and Dave Schuller and Don Cooper, are no longer with me. They are my regular partners Andy Gill and Marshall Dickman; my Maine men Jason Terry, Keith Wegener and Blaine Moores; and, my fly-fishing, head-shrinking, poker-playing, world-traveling buddies Steven Cooper, Elliot Schildkrout, Jonathan Kolb and Randy Paulsen.

Many other angling companions, too: Dick Brown, Skip Rood, Art Currier, Tom Rosenbauer, Barry and Cathy Beck, Jay Cassell, Phil Caputo, Rod Cochran, Rip Cunningham, Art Scheck, John Likakis, Phil Monahan, Joe Healy, Nick Lyons, Datus Proper, Ted Williams, Will Ryan, Tom Fuller, Spence Conley, Phil and Shirley Craig, Fran Verdoliva, Jack Gartside, Cliff Hauptman, Jeff Christenson, Rick Boyer, Andy Warshaw, Steve Wight, Mike Blaisdell, Bill Sheik, Hans Carroll, Paul Koulouris, Tony Brown, John Brady, Joe Phillips, Sam Downing,

Charles Poindexter, John Barr, Jim Smith, Ian James, T. L. Lauerman, Tom Murray, Jeremiah Gulley, Bob White, Gary McCown, Gary Pensinger.

And my father's partners who always included me: Harold Blaisdell, Ed Zern, Corey Ford, Lee Wulff, Put Putnam, Frank Woolner, Gorham Cross, Joe Bates.

And guides Bill Rohrbacher, Bob Lamm, Fred Jennings, John Gulley, Wayne Reed, Bob Bergquist, Martin Carranza, Gustavo Southart, Taku, Pancho, Neale Streeks, Brant Oswald, Mike Lawson, Randy Savage, Chad Hamlin, Jared Powell, Ben Floyd, Bob McAdams, Harry Lane, Phil Farnsworth, Ed Taylor, Walter Ungermann, George Smith, Andrew Cummings, Nat Moody, Sammy Knowles, Mike Hintlian, Fran Verdoliva, John Sharkey, Tony Biski, Denise Barton, John Berry.

And, especially, my wife Vicki, and my kids Mike, Melissa and Sarah, and my stepsons Blake and Ben.

Of course, there are countless others whose paths I've crossed in more than half a century on the water, and who've crossed mine, who have inspired me to look at my fly-fishing passions from unexpected angles and have thus inspired me to write about it.

These are true stories, or essentially true. I am scrupulous about avoiding exaggeration and falsehood, but I don't hesitate to reconstruct conversations or to condense experiences if doing so will enhance the Truth.

I have included here one short story in which fishing (but not fly fishing) is important, although not the point of it. Short stories are always about characters. If you want only Truth, you won't hurt my feelings if you skip the story.

Most of the pieces in this book have been previously published. Many of them appeared on the back page of *American Angler*, where I write the "Reading the Currents" column every issue. Several others were first published in *Gray's Sporting Journal* or *Field & Stream*. Editors Phil Monahan, James Babb, and Slaton White deserve all the credit—for their high standards, for their guidance, for their tolerance, and for their friendship, as well as for their uncanny editing.

Chickadee Farm
Hancock, New Hampshire
June 2006

PART I

Brookies, Browns, and Bows

"Trout are quite unaware of their exalted status."
—Harold F. Blaisdell, *The Philosophical Fisherman*

"A trout river is like a book:
some parts are dull and some are lively."
—H.G. Tapply, *The Sportsman's Notebook*

"Brook trout are generally considered to be far stupider than
brown trout. On the other hand, brook-trout fishermen are
probably no more stupid than brown-trout fishermen."
—Ed Zern, *How to Catch Fishermen*

1

Virtual Angling

I was leaning my elbows on the bridge rail watching the water glide under me and spread into a wide slow pool. It was that dusky time of day halfway between afternoon and night when summer trout streams begin to rouse themselves. I was late for supper, but I was married to a fly fisher and would be forgiven.

The low-angled sun slanted through the overhanging willows spreading a mottled patchwork of shadow and light upon the water. Some undulating pale mayfly spinners were dapping their abdomens on the surface, and now and then a few smaller, darker mayflies came drifting along—either the leftovers from a mid-day hatch or the heralds of an evening event to come.

Some cumbersome craneflies and neon damsels and fluttery caddisflies were flapping around the streamside shrubbery. Swallows and waxwings were swooping over the water. Soon the bats would come out to play.

Directly below me, in a patch of sunlight in the cushion behind the middle bridge abutment, a brown trout was finning just under the surface. I guessed he'd go fourteen or fifteen inches, a really nice fish for this particular New Hampshire stream. Periodically he'd sidle into the current seam. His dorsal fin would break the surface, his head would twist to the side, and his mouth would wink white, and then he'd ease back into his cushion. Eating emergers, I guessed.

Three other fish were lined up along the bank downstream from a sweeper on the deep left side of the pool. They were barely dimpling the surface—the kind of riseforms that sometimes betray really big fish, but could just as easily be made by two-inch chubs. I guessed—or preferred to believe—that these were trout. Sipping spinners, I figured, though it might've been ants or midges. I'd try a spinner first.

Down where the water quickened near the tailout two or three smallish fish kept splashing. A high-floating caddis skittered over them would do the job.

But my attention was focused on that nice brown behind the abutment. He'd be the trickiest one to catch, and he was therefore the most interesting. He was coming up regularly—about once a minute. A serious feeder. Assuming I figured out what he was eating and found a good imitation in my flybox, I'd need to cast it way up under the bridge to get a drift along that current seam, and to do that I'd have to wade nearly to the middle of the pool, where, I happened to know, the water would be lapping the tops of my waders. But unless I was standing in the right place, a braid of current at the bottom of the trout's cushion would grab my leader and drag my fly away from his feeding lane.

Even from the middle of the stream, the only way to beat the drag would be with a puddle cast. I'd have to tie on an extra-long tippet, drive it up under the arch of the bridge on a tight loop, and stop it abruptly. If I did it right, the tippet would land in loose coils and the fly would drift draglessly right along that trout's feeding lane, and if I'd tied on the right pattern, and if I'd timed it right, the fish would slide out of his cushion and drift back under my fly, and I'd see his back arch and then the swirl as he took it and twisted away, and I'd raise my rod tip and feel the fish's strength and energy surge up the line and through the rod to my hand.

"Hey, mister. Lookit that. There's a big fish down there. See it?"

I nearly jumped off the bridge. "You shouldn't sneak up on a fellow like that," I said.

He was a kid, twelve or thirteen years old, I guessed. He'd leaned his bike against the bridge and was now standing beside me, up on tiptoes, elbows on the rail, squinting down at the water.

"Of course I see the fish," I added.

"I wasn't sneaking," he said. "You just weren't paying attention. I think I coulda exploded a bomb under you and you wouldn'ta noticed. You were like totally in a daze or something."

★ ★ ★

My father took me with him from the beginning. When we went fishing, I was his partner, not his kid. I took my equal turn rowing the boat, paddling the canoe, or running the outboard motor, just as I tied my own clinch knots, baited my own hooks, and unsnarled my own backlashes.

Eventually I figured out that Dad had important life-lessons in mind, but at the time I understood that taking turns was simple and obvious fairness: Everybody, even fathers, would rather fish than paddle. It never occurred to me that some parents would let the kid do all the fishing, any more than I could imagine a father never bringing his kid fishing with him.

When I got older, my father abandoned his equal-time-with-the-paddle policy. "Just grab the rod, get up there in the bow, and don't argue about it," he'd say when we launched our canoe.

"We should flip for it," I'd say.

"I told you, don't argue. You're supposed to honor your father."

"We'll swap ends later, then."

"We'll see."

As often as not when I figured it should be his turn and suggested it was time for him to fish and me to paddle, he'd say, "Nah. You go ahead. I'm having fun."

After a while, I came to realize that he really *was* having fun. He liked maneuvering the canoe to give me an easy cast at a good-looking spot along the bank of a bass pond or a current seam on a trout river. He got a kick out of it when his guiding efforts paid off in a fish.

"It's just as much fun as fishing," he claimed. "It doesn't matter which of us happens to be holding the rod. Either way, I feel like an equal participant. It's not me or you casting the fly and hooking the fish. It's *us*."

"Fishing in your imagination," I said. "Virtual angling."

"Well, sure," he said. "Once you've packed away some experiences, it doesn't take much to roll out the mental home movies and to spark the muscle memories. When I see you holding a bending rod, I can *feel* it. When I watch you cast, the part of my brain that guides my casting arm is doing it along with you."

When he became too infirm to go fishing, my father insisted that I narrate detailed reports of all my angling adventures, great and small. He liked to hear about a summer evening on my local bluegill pond just as much as a week on an Alaskan salmon river. He'd close his eyes when I talked, and if I skimmed over some detail, he'd interrupt me. He wanted to know how the river smelled, how the breeze riffled the water, how the trout sipped the mayfly spinners, how the mist rose off the stream.

And if I did it right, I could tell that he was feeling and smelling and hearing and seeing it all for himself.

I used to think my father was odd. Who else would truly enjoy watching somebody else fish as much as he enjoyed fishing himself? How could a man who knew he'd never go fishing again genuinely love hearing other people's stories the way Dad did?

Well, we're all virtual anglers. We daydream of fish and rivers and hatches when we tie flies, when we take showers, when we drive automobiles. We join clubs and watch videos and attend shows. We devour catalogs and pamphlets. We hang around fly shops. We buy lots of stuff. We read magazines.

I know for a fact that you read books about fishing.

★ ★ ★

In the last months of his life, when I visited him, I usually found my father lying in his sickbed with his eyes closed and a little smile on his face. I'd sit beside him, poke his shoulder, and say, "Hey. You awake?"

His eyes would blink open. "I was fishing," he'd say.

★ ★ ★

As the kid and I watched from the bridge, that nice brown trout eased into the current seam, drifted backward, humped his back, twisted his head, and ate something.

"See that?" the kid said. "Too bad you don't have a pole with you."

"I've got a rod in my car," I said. "I don't go anywhere without my gear."

"So whyn't you go catch that fish, then?"

I tapped my temple and smiled. "Because I already did."

He narrowed his eyes at me. "Huh?"

"Virtual angling," I said.

2

Trickle Treat

After living most of my life within earshot of highway racket where city lights blotted the stars from the night sky, I finally did it. I bought a little farm on a dirt road in the New Hampshire hills. My new hometown has a post office, a cash market, a library, and an inn that has sheltered wayfarers since 1789. There's a sheep farm and an apple orchard and a couple of cornfields. That's about it for commerce.

Our town dump is officially called "The Dump." It's that kind of a town.

My neighbors own fly rods and shotguns and canoes. They raise goats and pigs and chickens. They park backhoes and tractors and pickup trucks in their barns. They read books and debate foreign policy and drive long distances for good theater and first-run movies and veal piccata, too, and they send their kids to college.

That kind of town.

In my new town, stone walls line every roadside. Old cellar-holes are scattered through the woods. From my windows I can watch whitetail deer, wild turkeys, ruffed grouse, red foxes, black bears, and packs of coyotes hunt and browse in my fields. Barred owls and sharpshin hawks sometimes come swooping down to chase the chickadees from my feeders.

It's that kind of town.

In my town, there are twice as many miles of dirt roads as paved. It's mostly forest and meadow and mountain and swamp. Rocky streams bubble through every crease in the hillsides. Pristine ponds nestle in every depression.

You could spend a lifetime tramping all those woods, driving all those back roads, and casting flies upon all that water. Unfortunately for me, I don't have a whole lifetime. But I'm giving it my best shot.

★ ★ ★

And so I was bumping down one of those nameless dirt roads on an August afternoon last summer, with my topo map on the seat beside me and my old seven-foot fiberglass fly rod in back, going slowly, exploring, getting the lay of the land.

At the bottom of the hill, a brook flowed under a wooden bridge. Naturally, I pulled over to take a look.

On the upstream side, the brook came curling out of the woods and wandered through some boggy marsh. It was barely a trickle. You could jump across it without a running start. It flowed slow and deep and shadowy against alder-lined banks. It reminded me of another trickle that haunted me when I was a kid, and haunts me still. That one was called Job's Brook.

Fifty years ago, before the suburbs sprawled, native brook trout lived in Job's Brook. It meandered through a big trackless bog two towns to the west of my hometown. Of all the places Dad and I fished when I was a boy, Job's Brook was my favorite. We hit it two or three times a year, and not once did we encounter another fisherman, nor did we even see a footprint or a gum wrapper or a cigarette butt.

Mostly the brookies ran from five to seven inches long, but once I caught a ten-incher from Job's Brook. It felt cold and muscular in my hand, and its spots glowed like drops of fresh blood. My father admired it, proclaimed it a trophy and a treasure, and told me to put it back.

Native brook trout, he made me understand, were rare and beautiful, and so were the waters where they lived. He didn't use the word "endangered," but his meaning was clear and prophetic.

Today, Job's Brook, the trout water of my childhood dreams, flows through a concrete trough behind a strip mall—reason enough to move to a farm on a dirt road.

In the summer months that I'd been exploring my new town, I'd cast flies upon all the water that I encountered. I caught bass from every pond—largemouths in the weedy ones and smallmouths in the rocky ones. Most of the rushing mountain streams were running low and warm, and I caught nothing from them. In a few, though, I'd found mixtures of browns, rainbows, and brookies that splashed happily at the foam beetles and bushy dry flies I floated over them. The browns and rainbows suggested that the brookies, too, were non-natives, but I was glad to find them, and I marked those little streams on my topo maps.

So I got out of my car, squatted beside this little nameless New Hampshire brook, and stuck my hand in the water. Almost instantly the chill ran up to my armpit and whispered, "Spring seeps."

On the downstream side, the brook opened into a pool, if you could call it that, before it continued its aimless journey around the rim of a horse pasture marked by a curving row of alders and willows.

The pool was about the size of the office in my new house—ten feet across, maybe. A big pool, by small-brook standards. Quite possibly the widest, deepest hole along its entire length, unless there were beaver ponds.

Where the current pushed against the left-hand bank of this pool, it had dug an undercut that exposed the roots of the alders that shaded it. If any trout lived in this little trickle, the oldest and biggest of them would surely live right there.

I captured half a dozen grasshoppers from the weeds beside the road, knelt on the bank at the head of the pool, and dropped them in one by one. The first five kicked and wiggled their way along the current seam, disappeared in the deep shade of the overhanging alders, then reappeared, untouched, and continued downstream.

The sixth hopper disappeared in a little splash under the alders.

That was good enough for me. I looked up and down the dirt road, went back to my car, and grabbed my old fiberglass stick. It was already rigged with an elkhair caddis on a short leader. I knelt at the head of the pool and flicked a little roll cast onto the current seam. The fly bobbed along, entered the shade under the alders . . . and disappeared in a spurt of water.

I lifted my rod. And laughed. A tiny fish came skittering across the top of the pool.

I held it in my hand, all four inches of it. It was a miniature brookie, already beginning to show its spawning colors. A beautiful little trout.

It wasn't a ten-incher. It was better than that—a truly wild brook trout, too small to have been stocked. It had been born in this water, and possibly it was a genuine native whose line of ancestors stretched back to the retreat of the glaciers. I doubted that anybody had ever bothered dumping hatchery brookies into this little trickle.

I slid the tiny fish into the water, hustled back to my car, stowed my rod, and got the hell out of there before anybody came along to see what I was up to.

★ ★ ★

When I discover a new trout trickle, I treat it like one of my secret grouse covers. I mark it on my topographic map, and when I visit it, I park my car half a mile away and skulk through the woods to the water. I resist the urge to brag about it, and since my father's not available, I invite no one to fish there with me.

Unless you take turns, there's room for only one fisherman on a trickle, and most of my friends wouldn't do it anyway. Catching a five-inch trout from a brush-lined brook you can hop across isn't for everybody. It's muddy, sweaty, buggy work. It's a slog through briars and bushes and blowdown. It's not contemplative or even particularly relaxing. It's on-your-knees, down-and-dirty, sneak-up-on-'em fishing.

You can't really cast flies on a trickle. You drift them, you roll-cast them, you dab them, you steer them along, and you end up leaving a lot of them in the bushes.

Exploring a slow-moving trout trickle with a fly rod taps into some age-old strand of my DNA. I feel sneaky and stealthy, predatory and primitive and infinitely patient. I don't get those feelings anywhere else, and I crave them.

★ ★ ★

So I returned to my newly-discovered brook the next morning and explored it to its source, right?

Actually, no. A day became a week, and then a month, and then it was winter, and I never did go back. I want to explain that life interfered, that I had appointments and deadlines and emergencies, that my car broke down or my back went out. You'd understand that, but it would be a lie.

The truth is, I've been putting it off. For now, I'm savoring the mystery of my unexplored brook. I'm letting it fester and grow in my daydreams. I imagine it will be like Job's Brook, and I'll raise some five-to-seven inch native brookies as I creep through the alders. I'll miss more than I hook, but I'll hook a few, and they will be beautiful. In my fantasy, I'll come upon a beaver pond about a mile into the woods. Half a dozen fat eight-inchers will be Hoovering mayflies off the surface, and I'll catch two or three of them before the others spook. Maybe one of them will stretch to ten inches, and I'll hear my father's voice, calling it a trophy and a treasure and insisting that I put it back.

Eventually, of course, I'll explore the brook and learn its realities, and it will no longer be a mystery. But for now, the daydreams are better.

3

Fishing for Stories

My father was an outdoor writer, and most of his friends were, too. As soon as I demonstrated that I could tie on my own flies and unhook my own fish, Dad declared me his Number One Partner. Whenever his friends wanted to go fishing with him, they understood that I came with the territory.

So almost from the beginning I got to hang out with writers of my father's generation, men such as Lee Wulff, Ed Zern, Harold Blaisdell, Joe Bates, Burt Spiller, Frank Woolner, Corey Ford. Household names for American sportsmen back then. To their vast credit, they accepted me, tolerated my youthful enthusiasm and awkwardness, even befriended me.

What a deal they had, I thought. They went fishing and hunting all the time—and they got paid for it.

When I started doing it myself, of course, I discovered that outdoor writing wasn't as easy as those old pros made it look.

Writers experience fishing with about twice the intensity and focus of non-writers. Not only do writers read the water, study the weather, observe the insects, experiment with flies and, in general, try to catch fish, but they also, with a different part of their minds, look for story ideas. Writers assume that every fishing trip offers a lesson, or an insight, or a new trick or tidbit of information, if only they are smart and imaginative enough to recognize it. Writers go fishing for fun, sure. But they also go fishing for stories.

For the writer, a day on the water that doesn't inspire a story idea, no matter how many fish are caught, cannot be a successful day of fishing. The writer understands that there will be such days. Sometimes nothing worth writing about happens. But sometimes the writer finds himself wondering if he's losing his nose for the story. This is scary. A writer without ideas is like a doctor without patients. Unemployed.

★ ★ ★

Several years ago Mel Allen, an editor at *Yankee* magazine, offered to pay me to go fishing on Vermont's legendary Battenkill River. "We'll put you up at a nice inn in Arlington," he said, "pay all your expenses, of course. Just write us a feature story that captures your experience."

"You want a *fishing* story?" I said.

"Well, yes," he said. "Fly fishing on the Battenkill. Slanted for our readers, most of whom aren't fly fishermen, of course. Not an article. A *story*."

He mentioned a fee. It was an offer no writer could refuse.

I was thrilled, right?

Wrong. I desperately wanted to refuse. What if I went fishing and nothing happened? The readers of Mel's magazine wouldn't care whether I caught some trout or got skunked. Mel wanted a story that transcended the technicalities of fly fishing, and he trusted me to find it.

I didn't need that kind of pressure.

In the end I accepted the assignment. If I didn't find anything to write about, I'd just pay my own expenses and tell Mel that I'd failed.

★ ★ ★

We agreed that I'd spend four days on the Battenkill in the middle of May. Prime dry-fly time. If nothing happened in those four days, nothing would happen.

For the first three days, nothing happened. I caught a few small trout. I mostly didn't catch anything. I explored many different stretches of river. I saw some wildlife. I talked to the people at fly shops, restaurants, gas stations. I interviewed the other anglers I met on the river. I learned many facts about the river and its history and its fish and its hatches. Nothing new. Nothing particularly interesting for the non-fishing readers of *Yankee* magazine. The Battenkill was overfished and undermanaged and unrestricted to kayaking and canoeing and tubing and other activities incompatible with fly fishing. A few big brown trout lived there, but not many. Mostly they were caught in April by local old-timers rolling nightcrawlers along the bottom.

I fished with a desperation that increasingly bordered on panic. I didn't want to let Mel down. I figured if I could catch one of those big brown trout, maybe I'd snag a story, and that became my goal: Catch a worthy Battenkill brown trout on a dry fly, catch a story.

The first three days: Nothing.

The fourth day dawned soft, still, misty. Ideal conditions for a mayfly hatch. The best possible conditions for locating a worthy brown trout. If it was ever going to happen, it would happen today.

I crept along the riverbank, scanning the upstream water, waiting for my instinct to announce: Here lives a worthy trout. I passed up two dozen promising runs and pools before I found it. Here the river twisted out of the misty forest, funneled through a rocky gorge, then widened into a long, broad pool. The current pushed against the high brush-clogged bank on the left. It was breathtaking. Classic.

Here I would make my stand. If nothing happened here, nothing would happen, and I'd pack up and go home without a story. I sat on a log and watched the water.

An hour passed before I spotted the unmistakable trout nose. I didn't move for ten minutes, the interval it took him to come to the surface four times. He rose in precisely the same place each time, right on the seam about two feet directly upstream from the uppermost sweeping branch of an arching oak tree. The only way I could float a fly over him was from the side and upstream.

His delicate riseform suggested that he had selected spinners to eat. They drifted inert on the water's surface, easy pickin's for an energy-conscious trout. I saw two kinds of spinners on the water—large rust-colored ones and smaller olives. Knowing the perversity of large trout, I guessed this one had selected the olives.

I found a good match in my fly box and tied it to my tippet. My hands, I noticed, trembled just a little. After three days, the Battenkill had showed me a worthy trout. Now it was up to me. The odds, I knew, were slim. Getting a drag-free drift would require a tricky reach cast and a big upstream mend, and I figured I'd only have one chance to get it right. And even if I hooked this fish, he would bolt to what I assumed was his lair under the tangled timber against the bank. My tippet was too slender. It would snap if I tried to hold him back. Otherwise he would wrap me and surely break me off.

Perhaps not. When they feel the hook, large trout sometimes shoot directly upstream, or try to slog it out in midriver, or exhaust themselves by jumping repeatedly. I might get lucky.

I focused on the first challenge, which was to wade into position to make my cast. A careless step would send warning waves across the quiet pool, and the trout would dart back to his hideout for the rest of the day. So I moved downstream and crossed in the quick water of the pool's tailout. Then I climbed the bank and pushed through the alder tangles to a spot directly across from the fish. I paused there until his nose showed again. Then I slipped down the bank and into the water.

The river spread about eighty feet wide here, and my trout lay about three feet from the far bank. To drop an accurate cast over him, I'd need to wade to midstream. I began to edge forward, shuffling my feet slowly, wary of making ripples. He rose again. As I moved closer I saw the size of his nose more clearly and mentally compared it to trout noses I had seen on other rivers. An eighteen- or nineteen-incher, I guessed. Not a Battenkill five-pounder. But a most worthy trout.

I had to resist the impulse to cast. I was still too far from him. One careless presentation would spook him. So I eased cautiously forward. He showed his nose again. He had established a rhythm now, and I had learned it.

A hollow thunk echoed from somewhere upstream, but it barely registered. I was focused on my trout. I was almost there. I began to strip line off my reel.

That's when the man in the canoe materialized out of the mist. He floated down through my pool, half-way between me and the place where my trout had been rising, thunking his paddle against the gunwale on every stroke.

"Any luck?" he asked cheerfully.

I shook my head. "Nope."

"Say," he said. "You got the time?"

I glanced at my watch. "Two-fifteen."

"Thanks." He waved. "Well, good luck, then."

The canoe's bow waves rolled toward the banks. I watched the man in the canoe glide downstream and disappear in the mist. The thunk of his paddle echoed back at me.

Then I reeled in, waded to the bank, sat on a rock, and thought about it. I'd been on the water for nearly six hours, all for one decent shot at that one trout.

I-the-angler could barely restrain myself from throwing rocks after the man in the canoe.

I-the-writer couldn't stop smiling.

I'd failed to catch a worthy trout. But I'd landed a story.

4

Hatching the Match

Around the time Vicki and I figured out that a match might be hatching between us, she asked me to take her fly fishing. She'd never tried it, but she'd seen movies with hunks such as Brad Pitt casting graceful loops over wild Montana rivers, and she knew I pulled on waders now and then. She thought fly fishing looked altogether alluring.

We went to a little panfish pond not far from my house in the suburbs. I led the way over the winding trail through the woods, and halfway down the slope I stopped short. A fat snake—a four-footer, at least—was sunning itself on the path. It looked like a boa constrictor.

"What's the matter?" said Vicki.

"There's a rather large snake in front of us," I said. "I think it's a milk snake."

"I . . . hate . . . snakes," she said.

"Indiana Jones," I said proudly. Vicki wrote a weekly column of film criticism. I'd learned to be alert for her movie allusions. Most of them were way more obscure than this one.

"I don't mind bugs," she said. "Worms and frogs don't bother me. But snakes . . ."

When I opened my mouth to speak, she pointed her finger at me. "Don't," she said. "Don't you dare lecture me about all the beneficial qualities of snakes. I don't care how harmless that one is. I don't like 'em."

"I don't like 'em, either," I said.

We detoured around the snake to the pond, and after some trial-and-error casting (with way too much nit-picky instruction from me, which she pretty much ignored), Vicki managed to flick a panfish bug upon the water. Pretty soon one of those generous bluegills sucked it in.

"You've gotta set the hook," I said when she didn't react.

"Huh?"

"Set the hook," I said. "Lift your rod when a fish strikes."

"Strikes," she repeated.

"Eats your fly," I explained.

"I was waiting for him to tug on my line."

The next time a bluegill slashed at her bug, I said, "Set the damn hook."

"You don't need to yell at me," she said. "I'm having a good time. I'm not an expert like you, you know."

I started to say, "I'm no expert," but I realized that wasn't her point, so I didn't.

A few weeks later, Vicki told me that she'd enrolled in the L. L. Bean fly-fishing school. It was quite sweet, the way she explained that she thought it would work better if someone other than I taught her, and I was pleased that she wanted to learn and that I hadn't already ruined it for her.

She came back from the school with an efficient casting stroke, the ability to tie a few knots, a solid, if rudimentary, understanding of fish behavior and aquatic entomology, and a fly-fishing outfit of her own.

For the rest of that summer, we spent many happy hours in my canoe casting panfish poppers toward lily pads and fallen timber and overhanging bushes. Vicki tied on her own flies, cast smoothly, set the hook gently but firmly, landed, unhooked, and released her bluegills, paused often to watch herons and ducks and muskrats, and insisted on taking her turn with the paddle.

For my part, I did my best to keep my mouth shut.

Once when she had the paddle, a four-pound largemouth engulfed the bluegill bug I was casting.

When I landed it and held it up, she said, "That was so cool, seeing you do that."

My thought was: I wish she'd been the one to catch it.

★ ★ ★

The following winter Vicki announced that she'd signed up for an all-female fly-fishing vacation out West with an outfitter called Reel Women. They were going to float the South Fork of the Snake and camp out on the river.

"I hope you're not doing this for me," I said.

She frowned. Her expression said: "Are you nuts?"

"I mean," I blustered, "I have a lot of fly-fishing friends whose wives don't fish, and it seems to work fine for them."

"I'm doing this," she said, "for me."

That summer, after her third day in Idaho, Vicki called me. "Hey," she said. "I caught a big one." Enthusiasm bubbled in her voice. "She was a cutt, almost nineteen inches. I spotted her rising at the tail of a riffle, and when I finally got a decent drift over her, she ate it. I did it all, except the guide netted her. It was way awesome." She paused. "I couldn't wait to tell you."

"That's terrific," I said. "What'd you catch her on?"

"Is it important?"

"Not really. It's just one of those fly-fishing questions."

"It happened to be a PMD parachute, size sixteen. Pale Morning Dun. A pretty name for a pretty insect." She took a breath. "I've made some wonderful friends. We laugh all the time. Yesterday we got caught in a hailstorm. Do you know where they got the name Grand Tetons?"

"Tell me," I said.

She did, and we both laughed.

"So are you having any fun?" I said.

"What do you think?"

Vicki has been taking a week-long vacation with her lady fly-fishing friends to various destinations in the Rocky Mountain West every summer since that one. There are countless long winter telephone calls as she and the friends she made on that first adventure on the South Fork lay plans for next summer's trip. I've overheard Vicki's end of some of those conversations. They talk about their children and spouses and pets and jobs and homes, and sometimes about where and when they should go fishing.

★ ★ ★

Last summer marked the tenth anniversary of the trip when Vicki and her fly-fishing gang of women first met. They arranged to hook up with Reel Women again for a float-and-camp reprise on the South Fork where it all began.

To honor this occasion in Vicki's fly-fishing life—and in our relationship—I decided to tie her an assortment of flies, all the flies she'd ever need for a two-day drift down the South Fork. I wanted her to be able to say to her guide: "Oh, I've got my own flies. My sweetie tied them for me. See?"

I consulted Linda Windels, the ringleader of Vicki's gang. Linda is as passionate and knowledgeable about fly fishing as anybody I know, and she lives close to the South Fork.

"We'll need tons of PMDs," she said. "Sixteens. On the South Fork their bodies are kind of pinkish. Emergers, of course, too. Don't forget Rusty Spinners. And we might run into some Baetis. Twenties and twenty-twos. Pheasant Tails and Hare's Ears, of course. All sizes. Um, tan caddis with a greenish body. I use peacock herl on mine. Don't forget terrestrials. We should see hoppers, and beetles and ants are always important. Woolly Buggers, naturally. What am I leaving out?"

"That sounds like a good start," I said.

After several weeks of feverish tying, I got an email from Linda. "I forgot to mention Yellow Sallies and Golden Stones," it said. "Toward evening there's also sometimes a little dark low-profile caddis, size 18, on the water."

The flies I tied filled two large boxes. I gave them to Vicki the night before she left for Idaho.

She opened the boxes and poked around with her finger, naming them. PMD. BWO. Caddis pupa. Midge larva. PT nymph. Yellow Sally. Sparkle dun. Hopper

Ten years ago she didn't know what a dry fly was.

"They're gorgeous," she said. She hugged me. "That's a lot of work. Thank you."

"I like the idea of you catching trout on flies I tied for you," I said.

"Me, too."

★ ★ ★

"It was great," Vicki said when she got back. "We laughed all the time. I fell out of the boat. The guides were terrific. Amazing food. I'd forgotten how spectacular that canyon is. It rained the whole first day and we got soaked. We saw loads of eagles and a pair of moose . . ."

"And how," I said when she stopped for a breath, "was the fishing?"

"Oh," she said, "it was pretty good. The water was a little high and off-color after the rain. The PMDs came off in the afternoon, but the fish weren't really up on them. I got a few nice ones, though, casting from the driftboat, hitting the seams and foamlines."

"What'd you catch 'em on?"

"Chernobyl Ants." She touched my cheek. "I wanted to use your flies, but Lori Ann thought . . ."

"Always listen to your guide," I said.

"I hope I didn't hurt your feelings."

I shook my head. "If you've got to choose between feelings and trout," I said, "go for the trout."

"Yes," she said. "You taught me that."

5

The Truth About Dry-Fly Fishing

Behold the dry-fly purist, with his form-fitting neoprene waders, bulging vest, expensive graphite rod, and fancy English reel. He speaks Latin fluently and spends more time studying insects than casting to trout.

He'll be happy to bore you with the hoary traditions of dry-fly fishing, its ancient and honored roots in England where it all began nearly 400 years ago, where they're called "anglers," not "fisherman," and where his counterparts still wear tweed jackets and old school ties and plus-fours and fish by the strict rules of the river: Upstream dry flies only, and only to rising trout. The sporting way.

He's proud of his skill, the years it took him to master the delicate art of the fly rod. He loves the beauty of those graceful loops his line makes as it rolls out over the water.

The purist insists he doesn't care about actually catching trout. He's above all that. He'd rather get skunked than demean himself by using anything but a dry fly. He's the Ultimate Sportsman, you see. It's all about the scent of clean air, the gurgle of rushing water, the symphony of birdsong. He loves dry-fly fishing for its ambiance, its roots, its difficulty.

For its purity.

Go ahead. Snicker. Say what you're thinking: "Pretentious," "effete," "condescending," "smug."

The stereotype persists. The dry-fly purist has heard it all. It doesn't bother him.

Actually, he's snickering himself.

★ ★ ★

The truth is, we dry-fly fishermen dress and talk and behave the way we do for the benefit of others. We aim to promote the image, perpetuate the myth. If the name-callers buy into it we're happy, because we've got a delicious secret and we don't want too many people to know it.

However, at the risk of getting booted out of the Fellowship of Purists, I'll expose our secret: We dry-fly snobs like to catch fish as much as anybody. Sportsmanship, tradition, artfulness, and aesthetic values have nothing to do with it

We happen to know that dry-fly fishing is the easiest way to catch trout. That's why we like it.

Sure, there are times—early in the season, usually, when the water is cold and high and discolored—when trout sulk on the bottom of the stream and, if they eat anything, it's a worm or a flashy spinner or a weighted nymph, fished deep and slow.

But trout are mainly insect eaters. They're most vulnerable when they're gorging on bugs at the surface, as they do at least part of virtually every day of the season under normal conditions. At those times, worms and spinners and even weighted nymphs are almost useless, but anybody with modest skill and a dry fly that even vaguely resembles the insect the trout are eating can catch them easily.

★ ★ ★

The singular advantage that we dry-fly fishermen have over everybody else is that we can *see* what's going on. There's no hidden, subsurface mystery to guess at.

Consider:

1. When they feed off the surface, trout betray themselves and their precise locations. We dry-fly fishermen *know* when we're casting to a hungry trout. This knowledge gives us the confidence, patience, and persistence to concentrate on our goal: To catch that trout.

2. We know that when trout are at the surface, their range of vision is limited. Because we can locate our targets, we can stalk them and, by approaching them from downstream, creep close to them so we can make short, accurate casts without spooking them.

3. When trout are eating bugs off the surface, there's little guesswork to selecting the right fly. We can see what they're eating simply by observing what floats past our waders. We don't need any Latin to choose an imitation, and we know that a general approximation is usually close enough. If they're feeding on big cream-colored mayflies, we simply tie on a big cream-colored dry fly.

4. We can see how our line, leader and fly drift on the water, so our mistakes are visible. If the fly fails to pass directly over the

fish, our cast was inaccurate. If it drags unnaturally across the surface, that tells us why he didn't eat it. Whatever we did wrong, we can make the obvious corrections until we see that we've got it right.

5. We can observe and analyze how the trout responds to our fly. If he sticks up his nose and sucks it in, we lift our rod, set the hook, and bring him in. Simple, efficient, fun. Foolproof, really. If he refuses a fly that floats directly over him without drag a few times, we know we must change flies or change tactics.

6. Even when trout aren't actively rising, they're usually happy to eat a dry fly. Drifting a bushy white-winged floater through riffles and pocket water is about as easy as trout fishing gets.

★ ★ ★

So the next time you encounter one of those dry-fly purists on the stream, tell him you're not impressed. You know his secret.

The fact is, if you're not fishing with dry flies, *you're* the true sportsman. You're the one who's doing it the hard way.

6

Last Call

When Joe called, I'd just come in from working Burt, my bird dog, on hand and whistle signals in the field beside the house. Burt was pretty rusty, and neither of us was yet in hunting shape. But the poplars and birches were turning yellow, and the swamp maples had already started to drop their leaves. Two days earlier I'd awakened to frost on the lawn.

"Let's go fishing," Joe said.

I found myself shrugging. "Yeah, well, I don't know . . ."

"Secret river," he said. "You'll love it. Full of big brown trout, and they're hungry and aggressive right now. Got a pair of twenty-inchers this morning on my way to work. This river's full of 'em, and nobody knows about it except me and a couple other guys."

Burt was sitting beside me with his head cocked, listening to my end of the conversation. I fingered a burr on his ear and pulled it off. "Twenty-inchers, huh?" I said to Joe.

"Yep. Busted off another one, looked bigger. You want to catch a twenty-inch brown trout, this is the place." He hesitated. "So whaddya say?"

"I guess so. Sure. Sounds good."

Burt rolled his eyes at me, then plodded over to his dog bed in the corner, turned around three times, and lay down with his back to me.

On the other end of the line, Joe was silent for a minute. Then he said, "What's this I'm hearing? Something the matter with you? Don't you want to go fishing?"

★ ★ ★

For the first half of my angling life, I lived in a state where the trout season closed on the last day of September and opened on the third Saturday of April. The idea was to protect fall-spawning brookies, the only species of trout native to our local waters.

It had been that way since the turn of the century, when they decided fishing had better be regulated before it was too late, and even though native brookies were virtually extinct in my state by the time I was born, the fishing season remained closed for half of the year.

It didn't occur to me to question this arrangement—certainly not to resent it. Even before I was old enough to venture into the outdoors, my father's comings and goings taught me that the sportsman's year turned according to logical and comfortable rhythms. To everything there was a season, and Dad took whatever the season offered. Landlocked salmon at ice-out. Trout as the days lengthened and the trees leafed out. Bass and panfish in the hot summer months. Grouse and woodcock in the fall. Ducks and rabbits in December and January. In the coldest, darkest months he tied flies and waited for the ice to go out again.

I learned those seasonal rhythms from my father, and they became my own.

Or maybe I didn't learn them. Maybe they were embedded in my DNA . . . or maybe even in the collective unconscious of my species. Those rhythms felt—still feel—utterly innate. I never believed that Opening Day needed to be legislated. The third Saturday in April and the last day in September were not arbitrary. Those dates came just about when they were supposed to come in the natural order of things.

Thirty-odd years ago my home state, acknowledging that there were no longer spawning native brook trout to protect, changed the regulations. No more Opening Day, no more closed season. Suddenly, you could go trout fishing whenever you wanted.

I barely noticed.

I still fish for trout from April through June when the streams flow cold and clear and the mayflies hatch. On summer evenings I paddle around my ponds, casting deerhair bass bugs among the lily pads and against the fallen timber, while bullfrogs grump and mosquitoes buzz and night birds swoop close to the water. As the days begin shortening in September, my thoughts turn to bird hunting. I spend more time working my bird dog. I hunt grouse and woodcock and pheasants in October and November while the leaves color up, turn brown, and fall. I set out decoys for waterfowl in the ice and snow of December. During the frozen winter months, I tie flies and daydream.

Then sometime in March, when the snow begins to melt and the earth to thaw and new buds are coloring the willows and maples, my thoughts turn to Opening Day of the trout season.

★ ★ ★

I didn't try to explain any of this to Joe. He's too young to remember when we had an Opening Day.

Anyway, I had to admit that I was kind of intrigued by the possibility of big autumn brown trout in a secret river.

We agreed to meet on Friday, still a few days before the bird-hunting season opened.

Thursday evening Burt followed me down to my tackle room in the basement. He sat there with his ears cocked and a hopeful look on his face. Bird dogs have a strong sense of how the seasons turn. Burt knew that his favorite time of year had arrived. When he saw me sorting through my fly boxes, he turned around and shuffled back upstairs. Burt knows the difference between a box of woolly buggers and a box of shotgun shells.

When I left on Friday morning, he didn't even follow me to the door.

It was a two-hour drive over back roads to our rendezvous at Joe's river. Along the way I found myself studying the woods. In the low areas, the leaves had started to drop from the alders and, on the hillsides, the poplars were ablaze. Chipmunks scampered along the stone walls. I made mental notes of brushy stream bottoms and overgrown apple orchards and tangly field edges—places where in just a few days a man with a good bird dog might find a few grouse or a flight of migrating woodcock.

I wasn't thinking much about trout.

★ ★ ★

Joe was waiting at the end of the dirt road. We dragged his canoe to the edge of the river, then I followed him so he could leave his truck at the place where we'd take out. In my car on the way back to the put-in, he told me that his river took an eight-mile loop through the woods, a stretch of water completely inaccessible except by a long hike through swamp and forest. "A long time ago they stocked it with brown trout," he said. "But you can only get at it with a canoe, and I guess not enough people fished it to make it worth continuing to stock, so they stopped. You won't find it on any of the lists the state publishes. Hardly anybody knows about it. The trout have thrived here. You'll see."

I thought about autumn brown trout in their spawning regalia. Buttery yellow bellies, blaze orange flanks, blood-red spots. The colors of October foliage in New England. The colors of the woods when you're hunting birds.

Back at the canoe we pulled on our waders and strung our rods and debated woolly-bugger colors. Joe said that for the past few weeks the water temps had been dropping about a degree every day. Pretty soon it would be too cold for good fishing.

We launched the canoe, and instantly we were surrounded by the silence of the river. No hum of traffic, no barking dogs, no clank of machinery. Just the soft breeze in the hemlocks and willows that lined the banks and the gurgle of water flowing over gravel and around boulders.

We stopped at Joe's favorite runs and pools, beached the canoe, and climbed out. We covered the water with our woolly buggers, casting, mending, stripping, lifting, casting again, and every few casts came the bump and tug of a trout. We hooked some, failed to hook many. The trout ranged from seven or eight to twelve or thirteen inches. They were fat and cold-bodied, and they quivered with pent-up energy in my hand, and gradually, as the morning sun sucked the chill from the autumnal air, it could've been May or June. I was fishing for trout again.

When we stopped to eat our sandwiches, Joe said, "There are some big trout here. Honest. I don't know where they are today."

"I'm having fun," I said. "I don't care."

By late-afternoon the sun hung low in the sky and long shadows were spreading over the water. I noticed that my fingers and feet had grown numb.

I was casting mechanically now, thinking about how good it would feel to wrap my hands around a hot mug of coffee . . . when my bugger stopped in mid strip. I tightened, felt the solid hookup, raised my rod, and a deep swirl opened on the water at the end of my line.

From behind me Joe yelled, "Oh-*kay*! About time."

It wasn't the twenty-inch trout Joe had practically guaranteed. But that brown trout was a fat seventeen-incher. A really nice fish.

I released it, bit off my fly, reeled up, and took down my rod. "Good way to end the day," I said.

A good way to end the season, I was thinking.

★ ★ ★

We were paddling down the river, Joe in the stern and I in the bow, heading for his truck at our takeout. The sun was slipping behind the hills, and a layer of mist hovered over the water, and long shadows were creeping out of the woods.

Suddenly Joe hissed, "Shh. Listen!"

I stopped paddling, and then I heard it, too. It sounded like a balky old engine coming reluctantly to life somewhere in the distance, accelerating from a hesitant thump-thump to a steady thrum, pausing, then starting up again.

It was ruffed grouse, drumming on his log—next to the laugh of a loon, nature's most haunting, evocative sound. I wished Burt could have been there to hear it.

PART II

Pass the Salt

"This salt-water fishing, it is for men with hard
stomachs—like sex after lunch."
—Charles Ritz, *To Me, At Lunch*

". . . there is great pleasure in being on the sea, in the
unknown wild suddenness of a great fish; in his life and death
which he lives for you in an hour while your strength is
harnessed to his; and there is satisfaction in conquering
this thing which rules the sea it lives in."
—Ernest Hemingway, *The Old Man and the Sea*

"It is easy to tell tourists from tarpon. Tarpon have
a narrow, bony plate inside the mouth on the lower jaw.
Tourists (especially in St. Petersburg) have both
upper and lower plates."
—Ed Zern, *How to Tell Fish from Fishermen*

7

Fear and Loathing in Belize— Part I

About four feet of Mason leader material was looped around Andy's bent knee. He kept fiddling with the Mason and frowning at the book he'd propped open on the table beside his bed.

I was sprawled on the other bed with a glass of Jack Daniels sitting on my chest. It was our first night on Ambergris Cay, our first night ever in Belize. That morning we'd scraped frost off the windshield for our drive to Logan Airport in Boston. We'd flown in a big plane and then in a small plane, and then a motor boat took us through narrow jungle channels to the lodge on the white beach where we got our first-ever glimpse of a turquoise tarpon flat.

We drank Belikan beer and dined on deep-fried conch with vegetables that tasted like sweet potatoes. After dinner we met our guide for the week, a round, middle-aged Belizian named Pancho. He had a gold tooth and a quick smile and a soft rumbling voice.

Andy asked him what we might expect for our upcoming week of tarpon fishing.

Pancho flashed his tooth. "Wind, mon. Mostly expect beeg wind."

"Well, there's always wind," said Andy hopefully. "Right?"

"Not always," said Pancho.

I watched Andy play with his monofilament for a while, then said, "What're you making?"

"Bimini Twist."

"Looks frustrating."

"It's fun," said Andy. "I love knots."

"So why this particular knot?"

"It goes between the leader and the shock tippet."

"Is it necessary?"

"Lefty recommends it," he said.

I knew you shouldn't argue with Lefty. "Make one for me?"

"You really should learn how to make your own Bimini Twist."

"I know," I said. "But I'm on vacation. I don't want to think about all the things I really should do. Make me a tarpon leader and I'll give you some of my Jack."

Andy shrugged, and I knew what he was thinking, because it had been his mantra ever since we booked our week in Belize six months earlier. *Tarpon fishing is different from trout fishing. There's no room for error. You gotta get it right the first time. You might get only one shot at one of these great fish, and you don't want to blow it.*

I'd read Lefty Kreh's book. Well, truthfully, I barely skimmed the long sections about knots. Unlike Andy, I don't find much romance in knots.

I mainly studied the photographs. There was one shot of Lefty unhooking a gigantic tarpon. It looked as if that fish could've taken Lefty's head into its mouth. I wasn't sure I wanted to hook a fish that big. I mean, I did, of course. But it was scary, too.

★ ★ ★

Wind. Pancho was right. It howled all day and all night. It ripped the surface of the flats, churned up the marly bottom, turned the turquoise flats brown, and drove the tarpon into the deep water. "Meester Tarpon don't like mud," said Pancho.

Each day played out pretty much like the previous one. We hunted for bonefish in the morning on the incoming tide, and we caught a few. Not many. They were hard to spot under the gray sky and wind-riffled surface. Pancho theorized that gray skies made the bones even spookier than normal.

After lunch, Pancho poled along the dropoffs and channels while Andy and I took turns on the casting deck peering hard into the water. We saw very few tarpon. For one reason or another, we never got a shot.

Back at the lodge, the ten other anglers submitted similar reports. A few hard-earned bonefish. Few tarpon seen, none jumped.

At night, the wind shook coconuts off the trees. They crashed on the tin roof like howitzers exploding.

After four days of it, I had no more adrenaline left. My knees ached from rocking on Pancho's casting deck. My head ached from eye strain. My spirit ached from diminished hope.

The afternoon of our fifth day was no different from the others. Pancho poled in the wind, and Andy and I took turns not casting from the deck. The first two days we'd swapped every hour. Then we made it every half an hour. Now fifteen minutes was plenty. When I was up there on the deck, I found myself daydreaming and looking forward to relaxing with a Belikan beer and a Colonial cigarette.

"We'll stake out here for a while," Pancho said. "Two channels comin' together here. Tide's right. Good place to see tarpon."

He drove his pole into the mud bottom and tied it off with his stern line.

Andy looked at his watch. "Your turn." He stepped down.

I sighed, picked up my 12-weight, climbed onto the deck, and went through the routine. I peeled line off the reel, made a long cast, and stripped it in, laying the coils carefully on the deck so they wouldn't tangle when the tarpon made his first hard run. Ha, ha.

I left a long loop of line hanging out of the tip of my rod, checked the point of the hook against my thumbnail, then held the fly between my thumb and forefinger. Locked and loaded.

I rocked and looked and daydreamed, and I was thinking it must be close to Andy's turn when Pancho hissed, "Tarpon! Two o'clock!"

I looked. Gray, corrugated water reflected a roily gray sky.

"Where? I don't see 'em."

"Comin' *at* us, mon. Three o'clock now. A hundred feet. Get ready. They *comin'*. Six. No. Seven of 'em. *Beeg* tarpon, mon. This is your shot."

Okay, no pressure. Right.

Where the hell were the fish?

Then I saw them. Black shapes, bunched together, moving like a single organism. They were closer than I expected. In half a minute they'd pass right in front of me, barely fifty feet away.

I threw my tarpon fly away from my body, false-cast once, loaded the stiff 12-weight, double-hauled, and laid the fly out there about fifteen feet ahead of the lead fish.

"Yeah, good shot," whispered Pancho. "Leave it . . . leave it . . . now *streep*. Yeah, keep streeping, mon. He sees it. He comin' . . ."

I saw it all happen, and I can still see it now, almost twenty years later, a slow-motion movie in my head, the dark torpedo shape, the third one back in the school, veering toward me, speeding up, then suddenly turning—

"Hit heem!" yelled Pancho.

Strip strike, I told myself, and with my rod pointed at the fish I yanked back with my line hand.

"Again. Hit heem again."

I struck again.

And that's when my tarpon launched himself into the air, and none of the pictures or movies I'd ever seen enabled me to fully imagine the power of that leap, or the size of the fish, or the sound of his gills rattling when he shook his head, or the crash his body made when he fell back to the water.

"Good job," said Pancho. "He hooked good. Corner of his mouth, mon."

"You bowed to him," said Andy, and I thought I heard shock and amazement in his voice.

Where did that come from? Strip striking, bowing to a leaping tarpon? I never did that before.

The fish jumped three or four more times within fifty feet of our boat. I heard Andy's camera clicking.

Then my tarpon took off across the flats. Not as fast as those bonefish we'd caught, but fast enough, and unstoppably powerful. I tucked the rod butt into my belly, held the rod high, and let the fish run against the drag of my reel.

Soon the backing appeared and the gray fly line disappeared in the distance.

Way out there on the flat the tarpon rolled.

"Gettin' air," observed Pancho.

He'd stopped running. When I tried to retrieve some line, the fish took off. More backing peeled away.

He stopped again. I began reeling, and at first I thought my fish was beat and I was reeling in the dead weight of an exhausted giant tarpon.

After a minute I realized that I was reeling in only the dead weight of a heavy fly line.

I sat down. Andy handed me a Belikan.

"Down and dirty, mon," said Pancho. "Gotta turn his head, show Meester Tarpon who's boss, get heem in fast. Your fly just wore a hole in his mouth. Too bad. That was a beeg fish."

I looked at Andy. "I guess I must've skipped one of Lefty's chapters," I said. "It never occurred to me that I'd actually have to know how to fight a fish that big."

He shrugged. "Live and learn. Next time you'll know. It was fun, though, wasn't it? I mean, seeing that fish suck in your fly, and then all those jumps?"

"It was the most fun I've had in my whole life," I said. "It's just . . . you know."

"Guys who fish for tarpon a lot," said Andy, "they just want to jump them. Find 'em, cast to 'em, hook 'em, get a couple jumps, and then shake 'em off, go find another one. That's the fun of it."

I've spent the last twenty years of my life trying to convince myself that letting that Belize tarpon get away because I didn't know how to fight him didn't matter.

But I can't help it: It would've been even more fun if Andy could've taken a picture of me unhooking a tarpon with a mouth that could swallow my head.

8

Fear and Loathing
in Belize—
Part II

The first time I went to Belize the wind howled for a week. Andy and I stayed in a lodge with ten other fanatical tarpon anglers, and in that entire week, twelve fishermen, supervised by six highly-motivated guides, jumped exactly one tarpon. That lucky angler happened to be me, although at the time I felt profoundly unlucky. It was the first tarpon I'd ever hooked. I had no idea how to subdue a giant fish, and I let it get away.

Thereafter, I bored as many people as possible with my own *Old Man and the Sea* story. The Big One That Got Away. Ho, hum. I knew it was a cliché, but I couldn't shut myself up. That fish was six feet long, and he came rocketing out of the water barely 40 feet from the boat. His big round eye was staring directly at me, and behind me, Pancho was murmuring, "Oh, *beeg* feesh."

Everyone kept telling me how great it was to jump a tarpon, how all the fun of it was in seeing those magnificent fish take your fly and then launch themselves out of the water, how actually fighting them was exhausting and bringing them into the boat was meaningless.

I believed all of that in theory. It didn't change the fact that I'd blown the chance of a lifetime.

★ ★ ★

Three years after my tarpon misadventure, Andy and I returned to Belize. This time, our goal was to catch a permit.

With my tarpon failure still burning in my memory, I did my homework. I practiced seeing, casting to, fighting and landing strong saltwater fish by sight-fishing for the striped bass and bluefish that swarmed my New England coastal waters. I tied a batch of permit flies. I learned leader formulas. I even memorized some knots.

I reread Lefty's book, and I read several other books on flats fishing. I studied magazine articles. I looked up everything Del Brown had ever said about permit. Brown had caught more permit on flies than anybody in history, and he'd invented the definitive permit fly, a crab imitation that he called the Merkin. Permit subsisted mainly on crabs.

Most people didn't know what a merkin was. Brown's wife did, though, and when she heard about Del's fly, she insisted he call it something else. So he tried to convince people to call it Del Brown's Permit Fly. As a result of this little marital controversy, anglers who normally didn't care about improving their vocabularies looked up "merkin" in their dictionaries. Naturally, Del Brown's permit fly is still known as the Merkin.

A man with a spinning rod and a bucket of live crabs has a good chance of catching a permit. Permit are usually smart enough to recognize the difference between an actual crab and a crab made out of feathers and hair and fur and lead dumbbell eyes. Permit come equipped with superior olfactory equipment. They feed as much by smell as by sight. Drop a real crab in the path of a feeding permit and he'll probably eat it. Drop a Merkin or a McCrab in front of that same fish, and even if you didn't corrupt it with a single molecule of sunscreen or insect repellent or fly-line dressing, the fish will take one sniff and swim in the other direction.

Except once in a while, for reasons known only to Mr. Permit, he will dart over and eat a fake crab. Not often. Catching a permit on a fly is universally considered the ultimate fly-rod challenge.

According to rumors, one guy who made a name for himself as a permit fly-rod expert collected a bucket of live crabs every morning before a day of fishing. He smashed up the crabs in the bucket and soaked his flies in the juice. Purists considered this cheating. Pragmatists argued that permit were so hard to catch that any edge was justified.

Pictures of this expert holding up big permit with crab flies in their mouths appeared in angling magazines with great frequency. He neglected to mention crab juice in his articles.

★ ★ ★

When we arrived, Taku, our guide, made a point of telling Andy and me that he was tied with Pops for the season's permit lead at the lodge. The guides took this unofficial competition very seriously. Their pride and reputations depended on how many permit their clients boated.

Taku was a smiling, easy-going young guy from Belize City, and when he saw Andy double-haul a crab fly into the wind, he laughed happily. When he saw me try it, his expression was more ambiguous. Crab flies are big and bulky and heavily weighted, and in the wind—that persistent Belize wind—throwing one on a nine-weight is like casting a sock full of sand, and it's a good idea to duck when you see a backcast coming at you.

It became apparent that fishing for permit really meant fishing for our guide's reputation. I wanted to catch a permit. But even more, I wanted to keep Taku smiling.

We hunted permit from the boat every morning. Taku poled along the deepwater flats, and Andy and I took turns on the casting deck, squinting into the gray wind-riffled water, looking for the blurry shapes of cruising permit or, even better, the sickle tail of a feeding permit with his nose down.

We decided to swap turns on the deck every time we got a shot at a permit, and for the first two days, each of us got several shots. Taku always spotted the permit before we did. Mostly we saw cruising fish that weren't particularly interested in eating, and more often than not, the plop of a Merkin sent them scurrying in the opposite direction.

On the second morning, a cruising permit turned and swam over to take a look at Andy's fly. Taku whispered, "Leetle streep." Andy gave it a twitch. The permit bolted.

When he climbed down off the deck, his hands were shaking and he was sucking in deep breaths. "Omigod," he said. "Did you see that? I think I'm gonna have a heart attack."

After two days, that was the highlight of our permit fishing. One permit's hesitant expression of interest, or curiosity.

That night back at the lodge, we learned that one of Pops' clients had boated a permit, dropping Taku into second place.

The next morning when we lugged our rods down to the dock, Taku was not smiling. Andy and I exchanged glances. The pressure was on.

We went to a flat where we'd spotted some permit the previous day. The wind chopped up the water's surface, and the sky was low and dark. When Taku turned off the motor and climbed up on his poling platform, I said, "Lousy conditions, huh? We'll never be able to see the fish."

"Conditions very good," Taku said. "Me, I can see feesh. Feesh can't see us."

It was my turn on the deck. I made a long cast, coiled the line on the deck, checked the sharpness of my hook. Adjusted my polarized glasses. Pulled down the brim of my cap. Ready to go.

Taku poled. Andy stood up in the middle of the boat, shading his eyes with his hand. We all peered hard into the water. All I could see was the gray sky reflected on the riffled mirrored surface.

Then Taku's urgent whisper: "*Feesh!*"

I looked around wildly. I saw nothing but reflection. "Where?"

"Eleven o'clock, man. Three permit. Noses down."

"I don't see them."

"Oh, jeez, I do," said Andy. "They're eating."

"Cast, man," hissed Taku. "Ten-thirty now. Fifty feet. *Cast!*" I still didn't see any permit, but I got my line in the air and dropped my Merkin at what I thought was ten-thirty, about fifty feet from the boat.

"No, no," said Taku. "*Left*, man."

I ripped my line from the water, false cast once, dropped my crab fly about fifteen feet to the left.

"*Right!*" said Taku.

I obediently picked up my line again and cast to the right.

"No!" screamed Taku. "I meant . . . he got it! *Hit heem!*"

I hauled back and felt the serious live weight of a big fish.

"You got him," said Andy. "Oh, wow. Big permit."

Permit don't jump. What they do is, they put their big flat side against you and they swim away, and no amount of sideways pressure can stop them, and in a minute that permit had taken all my line, and it was cutting sideways across the flat. I went down and dirty on him, tried to turn his head, remembering my tarpon fiasco when I failed to fight the fish aggressively, and after a minute the fish turned. I got my backing on the reel, and the fish surged again, and I hung on, and we were slogging it out.

Andy was laughing now. "When Taku said 'right,'" he said, "he meant you made the right cast. The fish started after your fly. When you yanked it away from him, he went nuts, and when you dropped it to his right he shot over and grabbed it quick before it got away. That was pretty funny."

Funny was one word for it. But "unworthy" was the word that kept echoing in my brain. I didn't deserve to catch this permit. I'd blundered and blown it, and the stupid fish had eaten my fly anyway.

I desperately wanted to land this permit. For Taku. For myself. For redemption.

After fifteen minutes, I'd retrieved all but thirty feet of line and the permit was near the surface, flashing his silvery side.

"He's beat," said Taku. "You got heem, man."

That's when my line went limp, and the permit righted himself and swam away.

"What happened?" said Andy.

I reeled in. "He's gone."

I glanced back at Taku. He was sitting on his poling platform with his forehead on his knees.

I looked at my leader, saw the tell-tale pigtail.

"Bad knot," I said. "That's what happened."

'Oh, man," said Andy.

Taku wouldn't look at me.

★ ★ ★

The next day, Andy landed a 14-pound permit. Taku was back in a tie for first place and smiling again.

★ ★ ★

A year later fishing out of Islamorada I brought two giant tarpon into the boat in consecutive days. They even announced my name on the local radio station.

I couldn't help thinking that I was a fraud.

9

The Line Storm

"It sure don't feel like fall's ever going to get here," said Keith mournfully. We were towing his Boston Whaler up Route 1, heading for the landing on the Kennebec to catch the turn of the tide. The back of Keith's truck was loaded with 9-weight fly rods and big-arbor reels and plastic boxes full of Deceivers and Clousers.

He flapped the back of his hand at the passing roadside. The birches and poplars were droopy and brown. In the swampy areas, the maples were turning the color of dead grass. "We got no pretty leaves," he said. "No frost on the pumpkin. No little russet fellers twittering down into alders on the full moon. The other day I ran Freebie through that string of alders along the brook behind Mrs. Sucheki's pasture? The mud was cement. No sign of a woodcock." He shook his head. "It don't even smell right."

"Bird season opens a week from tomorrow," I said.

"Wouldn't be surprised if they closed the woods," said Sam from the back seat. "I heard they might. On account of forest fires."

"Yeah, well, we could sure use some rain," said Keith. The summer-long drought had continued into September. We'd had no significant rainfall since Memorial Day, and this was another in an endless series of cloudless days. "Anyway," he said, "the good news is, the river's rumored to be full of stripers comin' down from Nova Scotia. The autumn migration. Maybe the fish know something we don't know. Be nice to intercept a couple of them big cows on their way south, put an end to this damn fishing season and get on to shooting ourselves some birds."

We launched the boat and headed down the river toward the estuary. Sam and I rigged up our fly rods while Keith steered. Sinking-tip lines, big Clousers with dumbbell eyes.

A minute later, Keith said, "*Hey*-lo." He kicked the outboard up a couple notches and swerved into a cove.

Sam pointed, and then I saw them. Swarming gulls and spurting water. We coasted up to the fish, and Sam and I both had our lines in the air. My first cast had barely hit the water when my fly stopped. "Got one," I said.

Then Sam grunted. He had one on, too.

Schoolie stripers pull hard. We never sneer at them. But we weren't after twenty-inchers. Sometimes big old cows lurk under the schools of smaller fish, and if the schoolies let a weighted fly to sink down to their grandmothers . . .

By the time Sam and I released our fish, the school had gone down. Keith putted around the cove, looking for spurts or swirls or wakes, and Sam and I dredged the water. But they were gone.

We headed back to the main channel. Now the tide was running hard up the river. Sam and I double-hauled our leaden sink-tips blindly against the rocks and along the dropoffs. The closer we got to the estuary, the harder the wind blew.

We saw no breaking fish. We tried to cover the likely water, the holes and rips and channels and current convergences where baitfish stacked up.

But it wasn't happening, and gradually my fishing adrenaline stopped pumping and my attention began to wander and my shoulder got tired and my casting deteriorated.

Two men throwing sink-tip lines and saltwater streamers tied on 2/0 stainless-steel hooks and armed with big lead dumbbell eyes into a hard quartering wind from a small boat is asking for trouble. An awkward double-haul, a sudden gust of wind, and my Clouser slammed into Sam.

"Ow," he observed. "You got me."

"I'm sorry, man. Damn. You okay?"

"I'm not sure," he said.

I put down my rod and looked. My fly had impaled the fleshy part of his right ear. The hook was buried halfway up the bend. "It's not bleeding," I said. "How's it feel?"

"Oh, fine," Sam said. "Pisser."

"Did you debarb that fly?" said Keith.

"I always debarb my flies," I said. I wiggled the big streamer that hung from Sam's ear. "That hurt?"

"Yes."

"Well," I said, "it looks like I didn't debarb this one. It's in over the barb, and it's not moving."

"Gotta push it all the way through, then," said Sam. "Okay?"

"Me?" I said.

"I'll do it," said Keith.

It was hard to watch. Ear cartilage is tough stuff.

"How you doin'?" I said to Sam.

"Good," he said. Then he grunted, and the barb broke through. I cut it off with fishing pliers, and Keith backed out the hook. Sam's ear gushed blood. Keith poured some beer over the wound, then gave the bottle to Sam, who took a big gulp.

"I'm sorry, man," I said to Sam.

He was holding an oily boat rag over his ear. "Don't worry about it," he said. "It could just as well've been me nailing you."

"Nice try," I said, "and I appreciate it. But I don't buy it. I got tired and careless, and I should've stopped casting for a while. No excuse."

"Look," he said. "It was stupid, both of us trying to cast at the same time. Sink tips and weighted flies in this wind? Dumb, both of us."

"I could've stuck you in the eye or the throat or something."

"Well, you didn't. So forget about it."

"You guys gonna keep beatin' your breasts," said Keith, "or do you want to go fishing?"

"You take the bow," said Sam.

"No," I said. "You go ahead."

Sam shrugged and began to cast. I sat down, snipped off my fly, reeled up, and took down my rod.

"What the hell're you doing?" said Keith.

"My arm's tired. I'm going to watch Sam, maybe take some pictures."

He arched his eyebrows at me.

I shrugged. "Okay, so maybe I'm just wishing fall would hurry up and get here. Fishing doesn't feel right anymore. I'm ready to go hunting."

"Not if we don't get some rain," said Sam.

Keith trolled and Sam cast and I watched until the tide turned. Nobody had a strike. Sam and Keith argued about whether the stripers were done for the season. Keith believed the year's southbound migration had already passed through the Maine coastal waters. Sam thought there'd be some more fish coming along.

I didn't join the discussion. I had no opinion.

★ ★ ★

The next evening I washed all of my fly rods, cleaned all my reels and lines, reorganized all my fly boxes, and stowed everything away. Then I took my 20-gauge Winchester Model 21 from its case, assembled it, peered through the barrels, snapped it shut, mounted it to my shoulder, and swung on the imaginary woodcock and grouse that were flying around in my den.

Then I wiped it off, disassembled it, and put it back in its case.

I sat in my big chair. Burt, my Brittany, ambled over and flopped down beside me. I reached down, scratched his muzzle and told him he better start giving serious thought to bird smells. I told him how the stripers were heading south. All it would take, I told him, would be a day or two of wind and rain to bring the woodcock down from Nova Scotia. A line storm, we call it in New England, the big blow that comes every year out of the northeast to demarcate the line between summer and fall. It was overdue.

And I told Burt how I'd impaled Sam's ear with a 2/0 Clouser that I'd inexcusably forgotten to debarb, and how I took that as a sure sign that it was time to put fishing behind us and move on to the next season.

That's when the phone rang. It was Art. He lives on the banks of the Merrimack River. "The river's full of fish," he said. "Schoolies, mostly, but a lot of big cows, too. I was out this morning, and—"

"No, thanks" I said.

"Huh?"

"No, I don't want to go fishing. Far as I'm concerned, fishing season's over. I nailed Sam in the ear with a big weighted Clouser yesterday. I already put my fishing stuff away for the winter. I'm ready to go hunting."

"Too bad," said Art. "They were breaking all over the river. We were catching 'em on Gurglers. Some pretty big ones, too. It was better than that time back in June."

"Better than June?" I said. "That was a helluva good day."

"This was better."

"The fish were pretty much gone from the Kennebec."

"Sure," said Art. "They're moving south. Now they're here."

"They were really breaking all over the river?"

"Everywhere," he said. "It was awesome. So whaddya say? Tomorrow morning?"

"Keith shoved that hook all the way through Sam's ear," I said, "and he didn't flinch. It must've hurt like hell. I could've put out his eye."

"Meet me at the ramp. Six-thirty."

"Okay," I said. "I guess so."

★ ★ ★

At six-thirty the next morning, black clouds hung low and dark and heavy over the Merrimack River in Newburyport. The air was still and moist and salty, and the water looked as flat and black as carbon paper. The muffled clang of a distant bell buoy echoed through the mist. I rigged up my seven-weight with a floating line and a debarbed Gurgler.

"Watch out for me," I told Art as we pulled away from the ramp. "I stick hooks into people."

"We've fished together for forty years," he said, "and you haven't stuck me yet. Anyway, I'm—hey!"

He pointed to a swarm of gulls that were circling and diving a hundred yards ahead of us. Under them the water was spurting into the air.

"Hit it," I said.

Art gunned the motor, then cut it, and as we drifted up to the melee of birds, bait and fish, I had my line in the air, casting over the bow, very aware of Art behind me in the stern.

My Gurgler hit the water. I made it gurgle, and it disappeared in a swirl. From behind me I heard Art grunt. I turned. His rod was bowed. Doubles on our first casts.

They were twin schoolies, not big, nineteen-inchers, but they pulled harder than any nineteen-inch rainbow or smallmouth and, when I released my fish and looked up, the air was full of birds and the water was bubbling with swirls and splashes as far as I could see. Every cast brought a slash and a strike, and we caught stripers steadily for two hours. Neither of us rammed a hook into the other guy's ear, and we didn't even notice when it started raining.

The fish disappeared abruptly and without warning. We cast for ten minutes without seeing a swirl or getting a strike. It was raining hard.

"It's over," said Art. "The tide turned, and that's that."

"Good," I said. I sat down, reeled up, and took down my rod.

Art peered up at the sky. "Lots of rain coming," he said. "Here's our line storm. Cold front behind it. Yesterday it was summer. Day after tomorrow it'll be fall, and the stripers'll be gone."

"Bird season," I said. "The woods will be wet. There'll be water in the brooks. The leaves will color up, and there'll be frost on the pumpkin, and the little russet fellers will come twittering into the alders on the full moon."

"Now you can stow away your fishing gear."

"I did that once," I said. "Thanks for making me do it again. Now maybe I won't have to think about Sam's ear all winter."

10

Stripers and Floaters

A SHORT STORY

My mother grew up on the Piscataqua River in southern Maine in the little town of Marseilles. They pronounced it "Mazell," same as the Maine town of Calais came to be pronounced "Caliss" and Madrid was "*Mad*-rid." Mainers did things their own way.

Visiting my grandmother in Marseilles fifty-odd years ago, when I was a kid, meant a long hot drive from our house in the Boston suburbs north on Route 1, which meandered through a lot of more-or-less identical little New England villages in coastal Massachusetts and New Hampshire. We always stopped for ice cream cones at the Howard Johnson's at the Portsmouth circle before driving over the Route 1 toll bridge into Maine. More often than not the drawbridge was up and we had to wait in a line of traffic for a tanker or barge to pass under. My father would let me reach out his window from where I sat in the back seat to put the dime in the palm of the toll-taker. It was always the same old guy, looking like he hadn't shaved in a week. I figured he lived there in his little booth, and I wondered where the bathroom was. He always said, "Thank you, suh," to me. His hand was grease-stained, and I could smell his sour breath even from the back seat of our car.

My mother's name was Hope. She had three sisters. Faith, Charity and Glory. I guess my grandmother ran out of virtues by the time she got to Glory. Jacob and Moses were Mom's older brothers. Uncle Jake and Uncle Moze. All of my aunts and uncles except Glory, the baby of the family, had many children—my cousins—and they all lived in Marseilles within walking distance of my grandmother's house. My uncles drove trucks and bull-dozers or had jobs at the Portsmouth Navy Yard. My aunts cooked and cleaned and raised their children.

My mother was the only one in the family actually to grad-uate from high school. Her sisters all had to get married, and her brothers quit school as soon as they were old enough to get jobs so they could chase the Marseilles, Maine version of the American Dream: Owning their own lobster boats.

Mom was the rebel. She went to college in Massachusetts, got her degree, and met my father, who had also gone to col-lege. They got married two years *before* I was born.

All that made my family objects of awe and suspicion among my aunts and uncles and cousins and their neighbors in Marseilles, and probably accounted for the fact that we didn't visit my grandmother more often.

As far as I was concerned, the best part of those trips to Maine was going out with my dad on Uncle Moze's lobster boat. Uncle Moze brought along a big tub of old fishheads that he used for bait. We chugged around the broad tidal river spewing diesel fumes, and Uncle Moze and my dad snagged the buoys with the boat hook, looped the thick line around the power winch, and hauled up the pots.

To me it was another kind of fishing. I liked anticipating what we might find inside the big wooden lobster pots. It wasn't that different from seeing my bobber start to jiggle and wondering what kind of fish might've eaten my nightcrawler. I was seriously hooked on fishing of all kinds when I was a kid.

In those days, lobsters were abundant, and Uncle Moze's pots generally came up crawling with them. He groped around inside the pot, came out grasping a lobster around its middle, and quickly measured it with his steel lobster ruler. He threw the shorts overboard, and the keepers went into a tub filled with seaweed. He tossed the crabs into a separate tub for my mother. She loved crabs. I can still picture Ma and Gram sitting at Gram's kitchen table cracking the shells and picking the meat out of a mess of boiled crabs and piling it in Gram's big glass punch bowl, with "Stella Dallas" or "Our Gal Sunday" playing on the kitchen radio.

My job was rebaiting the pots. I liked digging my hands around in the tub of smelly fishheads and stabbing them through their eye sockets onto the metal hooks inside the wooden pots. It made me feel useful.

After we finished hauling pots, we went fishing. Sometimes we dropped handlines weighted with big teardrop-shaped sinkers and baited with hunks of fish or clams into the deep water for cod and haddock and pollack and hake. As I remember it, we caught mostly dogfish. I got a kick out of feeling the vibrating little tugs from 100 feet down there and pulling up the line hand-over-hand, never sure what I'd find flipping around on the end. If it was one of those miniature sharks, Uncle Moze always grumbled and moved the boat.

When the striped bass were in the river, the men trolled plugs off the stern. My job was to watch the plugs churning along in the boat's wake and yell if I saw anything. I was too little to hold a rod. Uncle Moze would say, "You don't want to get yourself drug off the boat."

Those stripers were almost as big as I was. They engulfed the plugs behind the boat in a boil the size of a bait tub. They made the stubby boat rods buck and bend, and they zinged line off the level-wind reels, and the men whooped and hollered and cursed and groaned as they tried to bring them in. I knew better than to ask, but there was nothing I wanted more in my young life than the chance to feel one of those muscular stripers on the end of my line.

I liked catching dogfish on handlines, but striped bass were the fish of my dreams. I figured if I kept my mouth shut and did a good job rebaiting Uncle Moze's lobster pots, my time would come.

★ ★ ★

The summer I turned ten I figured might be it. During the long drive to Marseilles my dad kept teasing me about getting drug overboard, and when we got to the toll bridge, he let my little sister give the man our dime. I took that as a hopeful sign. Paying the toll-taker was for little kids.

When we arrived at Gram's house, Aunt Glory, the youngest of my mother's five siblings, was there. This was odd, since we'd gone to her wedding a few months earlier, and she had presumably moved into a trailer with her new husband, a pipe-fitter from Kittery named Norman who was quite a bit older than she. Aunt Glory was about seventeen that summer. She had curly black hair and blue eyes and a chubby face, and unlike my other aunts and uncles, she'd always treated me like an equal. We used to play Go Fish and Parcheesi and listen to rock-and-roll songs on Gram's kitchen radio. I hadn't seen Aunt Glory since she got married and moved in with my new Uncle Norman.

On this day Aunt Glory was sitting in a rocking chair on Gram's sunporch, just staring out the window. She was wearing a pink terrycloth bathrobe. Her arm was in a sling, and her eyes were red, and she was twisting a handkerchief in her hands, which were resting in her lap. Or, I should say, *on* her lap. Aunt Glory was quite pregnant. It looked like she was holding a big watermelon under her pink bathrobe.

I said "Hi" to her, but she didn't even look at me.

A minute later my mother and father came out to the sunporch. Mom looked at me and said, "We want to talk to Aunt Glory for a minute, Sweetie," which meant she wanted me to leave.

I went into the other room, but I could hear the murmur of voices, my mother's and father's and Aunt Glory's.

Mom said: "He did that to you?"

Aunt Glory: "Ayuh."

Dad: "Sonofabitch. He kicked you out?"

Aunt Glory snuffled.

Mom: "Because of that?" I imagined she was pointing at Aunt Glory's belly.

Aunt Glory: "He was drunk. Called me a whore."

Mom: "And when was this?"

Aunt Glory: "Four, five weeks ago, I guess."

Mom: "You're not planning to go back, are you?"

Aunt Glory: "He's my husban'. What'm I spose to do?"

Mom: "You talked to him?"

Aunt Glory: "Not since then. Moze and Jake went over a couple times, but Norman ain't been home."

Dad: "You better get yourself a lawyer."

About then Gram called from the kitchen, said she had corn chowder with oyster crackers for lunch for me and my sister, so I didn't hear any more about Aunt Glory. Gram's corn chowder was my favorite food in the world.

I was just finishing up my second bowlful when Uncle Moze came stomping in. He was a big man with a face like a hatchet. He was wearing black rubber hip boots folded down at his knees and blue jeans and a blue work shirt rolled up over his elbows. He said, "Hiya, Tiger," and punched me on the shoulder. "Gonna help me haul pots?"

"You bet," I said.

"Stripers're in the river," he said, "and the tide'll be about right. Where's your old man?"

I jerked my head in the direction of the sunporch, and Uncle Moze went out there.

I went outside and leaned against Uncle Moze's pickup truck so they wouldn't forget me, and after a while he and my dad came out. They were muttering to each other, and I heard Uncle Moze say, "Always was a good for nothin' sumbitch." Then he looked up and saw me and said, "Climb in back, Tiger."

So I hoisted myself up into the bed of the truck and found a place to sit amidst the tub of fishheads, the fistful of boat rods all armed with big plugs, the stack of old lobster pots with moss growing on them, the big coil of thick rope, and the case of Narragansett beer.

When we got to the cove where Uncle Moze kept his lobster boat moored, we lugged the stuff from the truck to his dinghy, piled in, and rowed out to the boat, and pretty soon the powerful diesel engine was thrumming and we were chugging out into the bay. Uncle Moze's lobster boat was broad-beamed and chunky and solid. It didn't go very fast, but you had the feeling it would just plow straight through a hurricane.

Pretty soon we came to the area where Uncle Moze put out his pots, and for the next couple of hours we were busy hauling them in, culling out the lobsters and crabs, rebaiting them, and pushing them back into the water. We ended up with an empty bait tub and two other tubs full of seaweed and lobsters and crabs.

Then my dad picked up one of the rods, unhooked the plug from the first guide, dropped it over the side, and let it free-spool back until it was about a hundred feet behind the boat. Uncle Moze cut back the engine until we were barely moving.

"Keep an eye out for birds," he said to me.

Maybe ten minutes later, while I was scanning the horizons hoping to spot a cloud of gulls diving at the water, my father grunted. I looked back in time to see the big hole in the water where the plug had been. Uncle Moze threw the engine into neutral, and Dad heaved up on the rod, lowered it, reeled up, and heaved again, and after a while the big striper came silvering alongside. Uncle Moze reached down with the gaff and levered the monster into the boat. It was close to four feet long.

Uncle Moze and my father were grinning.

Then, almost as fast as my dad could reel them in, there were four more of those three- and four-foot stripers flopping in the bottom of the boat. Fish were boiling and sloshing all over the river, and the air was alive with squawking, diving gulls and terns.

Uncle Moze said, "Hey, Tiger. Git yerself a plug out there, why dontcha."

I glanced at my dad, and he nodded. "Don't get drug overboard," he said. "Your mother would kill me."

I made a muscle for him, then picked up a rod, and I was just about to unhook the red-and-white plug and drop it off the stern when Uncle Moze muttered, "Now what the hell?"

I looked up. Another lobster boat had cut across our wake and was coming up beside us. The guy at the wheel was wearing yellow rubber overalls and a long-billed fisherman's cap. He was waving his arms and yelling, but over the drone of the engines I couldn't hear what he was saying.

Uncle Moze said, "Keep that plug in the boat, Tiger." He put the engine in neutral, and a minute later the other boat slid alongside. My dad reached out and held onto it.

Uncle Moze looked at the guy in the yellow overalls. "Damn it anyway, Lyle. What're you doin'? We was into stripers."

"Got us a floater," said Lyle. "You ain't got a radio, do you?"

Uncle Moze shook his head.

"Me neither," said Lyle. "I'm gonna go git the Coast Guard. You better head over there and stay with the damned body."

"Well, shit," said Uncle Moze. "They was bitin' awful good."

Lyle went up on tiptoes and looked into our boat, where our five giant striped bass were laid out side by side like big hunks of cordwood. He whistled. "Damn," he said. "Well, it cain't be helped." He pointed off toward the shore. "He's over by them reeds. I tied a buoy onto him. Tide's gonna start runnin' pretty soon. You better git over there so he don't git washed away."

Lyle put his engine into gear, gave us a wave, and headed across the river to the New Hampshire side where the Coast Guard station was. Uncle Moze steered us to where Lyle had pointed.

He slowed down as we approached the reedy shoreline, and then my dad said, "Jesus Christ," and then I saw it. I'm not sure I would've known it was a man's body if Lyle hadn't said it was. He was floating on his belly with his face in the water and his arms and legs sort of dangling just under the surface, so that just his back was out of water. He looked like a big white turtle. He was wearing a white sleeveless T-shirt and khaki-colored pants, and the skin on his neck and face and shoulders was shiny and swollen and white as lard. A crab had latched onto the side of his face, just under the water's surface, and some seaweed was hooked around one of his legs. Lyle's buoy was looped around the other leg.

My dad leaned close to Uncle Moze and whispered something to him.

"Ayuh," I heard Uncle Moze say. "That's fuckin Norman all right."

We idled there beside Uncle Norman's body for a few minutes, and then Uncle Moze said to my father, "Tide's takin' him out. Better gaff him."

So my father picked up the long-handled gaff we used for bringing stripers aboard, reached out, and tried to hook it around Uncle Norman's swollen leg. The sharp curved point sank right in, and I could see little pieces of flesh puff off and form a greenish-white cloud in the water.

"Don't look," my dad said to me over his shoulder.

Fat chance of that.

We drifted in Uncle Moze's boat with Uncle Norman's dead body for nearly an hour before the Coast Guard boat came speeding across the river and pulled alongside of us. Uncle Moze seemed to know the Coast Guard men, and they talked for a while. Then my dad unhooked the gaff from Uncle Norman's leg, and Uncle Moze started up the engine, and we pulled away.

I watched over the stern as they dragged the bloated body over the transom of the Coast Guard boat.

By then the tide had turned and the birds had disappeared. We trolled around the bay for a while—I got to hold a rod—but the fish were gone. So Uncle Moze headed in, and we moored his boat, loaded the lobsters and crabs and stripers into his dinghy, and rowed to shore.

★ ★ ★

I got a lot of attention when I told my friends back home about finding my Uncle Norman's body in the Piscaquata River. In my version of the story, I was the one who spotted the floater, and it was I who rammed the gaff through his leg and held on until the Coast Guard arrived. The girls, especially, loved hearing my story.

★ ★ ★

My family didn't get back to Marseilles, Maine again that summer, and the following summer when we went out to help Uncle Moze haul his pots, he said the stripers weren't in. We trolled plugs around the river for a couple hours anyway, my dad and I each holding a rod, but we never had a hit.

The next few summers when we went out with Uncle Moze, we handlined for cod and caught mostly dogfish. The stripers were pretty much gone, Uncle Moze said, and it was a waste of time to bother fishing for them.

★ ★ ★

My father explained it to me several years later:

When the Coast Guard hauled Uncle Norman's body onto their boat, they saw what appeared to be a bullet hole in his forehead. Forensic science wasn't very sophisticated back then, and anyway, nobody had much tolerance for a drunk who'd break his pregnant wife's arm. They never did catch whoever shot him.

I remembered that Uncle Moze hadn't seemed at all surprised when the floater turned out to be Uncle Norman.

★ ★ ★

By the time the stripers came back into New England waters, Gram and Uncle Moze had died, and Aunt Glory had moved to Florida with her third husband, and I had kids of my own.

Whenever I took them out on a boat, I let them hold a trolling rod no matter how little they were. I figured it was better to risk them getting drug overboard than to miss the chance entirely. Besides, you never knew when a dead body would show up and spoil it all.

PART III

Flies and Gear

"The most indispensable item in any fisherman's equipment is his hat. This ancient relic, with its battered crown and well-frayed band, preserves not only the memory of every trout he caught, but also the smell."
—Corey Ford, "Tomorrow's the Day"

". . . neither time nor repetition has destroyed the illusion that the rise of a trout to a dry fly is properly regarded in the light of a miracle."
—Harold F. Blaisdell, *The Philosophical Fisherman*

"You can transform a wet fly into a dry fly by rubbing it briskly with a Turkish towel."
—Ed Zern, *How to Catch Fishermen*

11

The Pink Sarah

I was sitting at my fly-tying desk tying PMDs and BWOs and Tricos for my summer trip, with frequent daydreamy pauses to gaze out the window at the snowy New England landscape. Montana seemed eons and continents away, but creating a dry fly and visualizing some fat spring-creek rainbow sucking it in made it feel closer.

I don't know how long Sarah had been there before I became aware of her. She'd dragged a chair up behind me and was sitting cross-legged on it, her elbows on her knees, her chin in her hands, watching me with those huge brown six-year-old eyes.

I took the fly out of the vise, bounced it on my palm, and showed it to her. "What do you think?" I said.

She poked it with her finger. "It's very small," she said. "What do you call it?"

"It's a Pale Morning Dun."

"That's a pretty name," she said. "Do you think a fish will eat it?"

"I hope so. It's supposed to imitate an insect that they like to eat."

She squinted at the little dry fly. "It doesn't look like an insect to me."

"That's because you're smarter than a fish." I patted my lap. "Want to make one?"

She shook her head. "I don't know how."

"I'll show you. We'll make a big one for catching a really big fish."

She shrugged. "Okay."

She scrambled up onto my lap, and with my arms around her and my cheek touching her cheek and my fingers guiding her fingers, we wound some thread onto a big streamer hook. We tied on a marabou tail, we wound on some chenille, we palmered a big hackle feather over it, and we tied off the head with a few half hitches.

I unclamped the vise and dropped our Woolly Bugger into Sarah's hand. "Your first fly," I said.

She shook her head. "This isn't mine. You mostly made it, not me. Besides, it's black. I don't like black. Black is boring. Can I make my own?"

"Sure. The first thing to do is select the ingredients. Decide what you want your fly to look like."

"I want it to be pretty." She rummaged through the piles of stuff on my desk and came up with a pink marabou plume, some orange chenille, and a chartreuse hen-hackle feather.

I talked her through it, reminding her to keep tension on the thread, now and then showing her how to execute a step and then unwinding it so she could do it herself, and she managed to get everything lashed onto the hook more-or-less all by herself.

When she was done, she unclamped the vise and held her creation in her hand. She grinned at me. "Do you like it, Daddy?"

It was, of course, misshapen and lumpy and asymmetrical, not even to mention garish.

"Your very first fly," I said. "I love it. It's quite beautiful. You should give it a name."

She squinted at it. "It's really kind of ugly," she said, "except for the colors. I think I'll call it the Pink Sarah."

"That's a pretty name."

"Do you think a fish would ever eat it?" she said.

"This Pink Sarah," I said, "will definitely catch a fish."

★ ★ ★

The smells—mothballs-and-feathers, tacky head cement, blue-dun dye bubbling on the stove—are evocative for me still. So are the names junglecock and golden pheasant and peacock, tinsel and floss and chenille, bucktail and hare's mask and marabou, badger and ginger and grizzly. After half a century, I still can't sit down to tie a fly without remembering . . .

In my family, the fly-tying season opened the day after the duck season closed, and it ended when the ice went out on Sebago Lake to signal the beginning of landlocked salmon fishing. Every year on New Year's Day, my father set up his fly-tying bench in the living room. Dad tied flies just about every winter evening. When I was a boy, I liked to pull up a chair by his elbow to watch him tie while our old Philco radio played big-band music in another corner of the room.

After dinner, he unpacked the materials for the evening from the big green breadbox he stored them in, and I soon learned that the brown bucktail and the skein of yellow chenille meant an evening of Dark Tigers, while the grizzly and ginger necks and the woodduck flank feathers meant that a couple dozen Nearenufs, Dad's version of the Adams, would magically emerge from his vise. When he took out the big hooks and the deer hides, I knew it would be an evening of "hedge-trimming"— spinning and clipping deerhair bass bugs.

He never used a bobbin. He stripped off a few feet of tying silk, ran it through his ball of beeswax, and used a half-hitch to secure the thread after every operation. He spread a dish towel on his lap to collect the trimmings, and after a session at the bench, he folded up the towel, went out to the back porch, and flapped the clippings onto the snow. "The birds will find it when the snow melts," he said. "They'll use it for their nests."

He was right. Come spring, I liked to wander around the yard looking for the bird nests. Usually they had strands of yellow chenille and silver tinsel and scraps of bucktail and feathers woven into them.

My father supplied his non-tying friends with flies, and since he had many friends, every winter he tied tens of dozens of flies—flies for every angling occasion, flies that his friends requested, flies for his friends' friends. Nobody paid him, nor did he want them to. They gave him back in companionship what he gave them in flies.

For a while in the early 1940s he tied commercially. "Three for a dollar was the going rate," he once told me. "It was a hard way to make money, and I didn't do it for very long. My problem was, I'm a perfectionist. I refused to sell a fly with any flaw, even if no one would notice it except me. But I learned a lot about fly tying that way, and I ended up with an awful lot of flawed flies. They all caught fish."

Dad considered fly tying to be a manufacturing process. But to me, what he did was an art, and the pieces he created were beautiful—perfectly symmetrical and proportioned, smoothly tapered, subtly colored. When I watched him, he made it look easy.

As the winter nights passed, his boxes filled with flies. When I was a kid, there were very few evenings when Dad didn't put in an hour or two at the vise.

And if I sat there quietly and waited long enough, he'd eventually pat his knee and invite me to climb up and tie a fly of my own. I'm positive I was the only kid in my first-grade class who could roll a woodduck wing and wind a hackle feather and make a whip-finish.

My flies never looked like Dad's, as hard as I tried. The wings always flared out at odd angles, and the heads came out big and lumpy. But, when I finished my evening's fly and took it from the vise and handed it to my father, he always held it up, squinted at it, poked it with his finger, and then handed it back to me. "Yup," he always said. "This one'll catch fish, all right."

Through the months of the fly-tying season, my own little box of flies slowly filled, and when the fishing season arrived, I tried them and discovered that Dad was right: As flawed and amateurish and outlandishly designed as my creations were, they did catch fish.

I gradually figured out that anything would catch fish if you tied it on and kept it in the water long enough, a principle that continues to guide my fly-fishing strategies to this day.

★ ★ ★

My father tied flies for his friends and for his own entertainment well into his eighties, even after he'd grown too lame and wobbly to wade a stream or paddle a canoe.

Then came the day when he bequeathed what was left of his fly-tying materials to me. "Take it all," he said, waving the back of his hand at the old green breadbox. "I can't use it anymore."

"You sure?" I said.

He held up his gnarled, arthritic fingers and shrugged.

I knelt down and opened the breadbox. I rummaged through the bags and boxes and envelopes and found junglecock and golden pheasant and peacock, tinsel and chenille and floss, blue-dun and ginger and grizzly necks. I sniffed the mothball-scented deerhair and hare's mask and bucktail. It was hard to imagine my father not tying flies.

★ ★ ★

The summer she turned seven, I paddled along the shoreline of a Maine bass pond while Sarah, in the bow seat, trolled, gripping her fiberglass fly rod in both hands.

When the fish struck and her rod bent, she squealed.

I landed the foot-long smallmouth with the gaudy fly in its mouth and held it up for her to see. "She ate your Pink Sarah," I said. "I told you it would catch a fish."

Sarah smiled. "I really didn't believe you."

"You should always believe your daddy," I said.

12

The X Factor

On a Friday in mid-July Marshall Dickman and I waded the Farmington River in north-central Connecticut. It took us a while to figure out that the trout in the Church Pool were sipping tiny olive spinners. I mean, these bugs were minuscule. About size 28. I found a few 26s in my box, but I couldn't poke my 6X tippet through the eye of the hook. I had to step down to 7X to tie on the fly.

Most of those foot-long brown trout squinted at my offering and proclaimed the fly too big and the tippet too coarse. A helpful Farmington regular I talked with in the parking lot afterwards told me you really needed to go down to 8X for these fish.

A few days and about 1500 miles later, I found myself drifting on a glassy lake in the wilds of Labrador casting a size 8 brown drake spinner knotted to a 2X tippet into the paths of some cruising six-pound brook trout and Arctic char. Caught a couple of them, too. The guide said a lot of his clients used 0X, and as far as he could tell, it didn't bother the fish.

From 7X to 2X in consecutive trout-fishing days. It got me to thinking about tippets.

★ ★ ★

As far as I know, I never fished with tippets made from silkworm gut, although gut tippets were still being used in my earliest angling days. I didn't pay much attention to what my father tied onto the end of my line when I first went fishing with him.

Over 50 years ago, when I began setting forth on my own for an afternoon of trout fishing, I carried a couple packets of nylon tippets in my vest. Not spools of material, but glassine envelopes containing separate coils of tippet. Each tippet was about sixteen inches long.

The post-war nylon tippets were not radically different from what anglers accustomed to gut expected. They were short, kinky, and weak. Pre-cut lengths of nylon stubbornly retained their springy coils when removed from their packets. Gut tippets had to be softened by soaking in water before they could be used and had been limited in their length by the capacity of the silkworm. The new synthetic stuff broke quite easily, too.

Back then, I changed or added tippet as infrequently as possible, mainly because tying blood knots challenged me. By the end of the day, after a normal number of bust-offs and fly changes, I might have a three-inch stub of tippet left. If it was long enough to tie a fly to, as far as I was concerned, it was long enough.

The Surgeon's Knot revolutionized fly fishing for me.

In those early days of synthetics, nylon leader tippets—even those from the same packet—varied wildly in their strength. The strongest of them wasn't very strong. Generally I never tied on anything finer than 3X. "Going down to 4X" was a radical move reserved for extraordinary situations.

Some fishermen liked to brag about "going down to 4X," as if the mere act of tying on such risky material was a sign of their superior expertise. It always seemed to me that "going down to 4X" was pretty much an affectation.

It's possible that my present aversion to 7- and 8X tippets derives from my fear that people will think I'm showing off.

Back then, I don't believe they even manufactured tippets thinner than 4X. I never heard anyone boast about "going down to 5X."

I caught plenty of trout on 3X. Busted some off, too. Nowadays, I rarely fish dry flies on anything thicker than 4X. It's tempting to think that today's trout are smarter and spookier and endowed with better eyesight than those of my youth, but I doubt it. Most of the trout we catch in New England waters these days were born in hatcheries, just as they were 50 years ago.

Maybe back then I got away with coarse tippets (by today's standards) because our main New England mayfly hatches—Hendricksons, Light Cahills, Quill Gordons, March Browns, Green and Brown Drakes—are large bugs, none smaller than Size 14. You still need 3X for these big flies.

The optimum tippet size is determined by the size of the fly, not the wariness of the trout. Flies tied on big hooks need thick tippet to turn them over, while you can thread only slender tippets through the eyes of tiny flies.

There's a mathematical rule for it called "The Rule of Four." Divide the hook size by four to get the optimum tippet size (or multiply the tippet size by four to get the fly size, although I can't think of an instance where you'd do it that way). So if you need to tie on a size 16 parachute Adams to match the bugs that are on the water, 16 divided by 4 tells you that you should be using a 4X tippet.

A 3X tippet is just right for a Size 12 March Brown. For a Size 8 Eastern Green Drake, use 2X.

For little flies—size 18 and smaller—tippet size isn't crucial. I use 5- or 6X interchangeably, and 7X reluctantly.

You don't reduce drag or fool sharp-eyed trout by "going down to" finer tippets. You do it be lengthening them. Follow the Rule of Four to determine the proper tippet size. To combat drag, tie on four or five feet of it.

I suspect that fifty years ago we ignored, or were unaware of, olives and sulfurs and tricos, not to mention jassids and beetles and ants—the tiny mayflies and terrestrials that, I assume, were eaten by trout back then just the way they are today—simply because tiny hooks and slender tippets were not widely available back then. A 3X tippet won't fit through the 6X eye of a size 22 dry-fly hook, which probably discouraged manufacturers from producing hooks that small in the first place.

The development of thin, strong tippet material made the mass production of tiny hooks feasible. The availability of small hooks, in turn, enabled anglers to "discover" tricos and blue-winged olives, midges and microcaddis, ants and jassids, and to tie flies to imitate them.

★ ★ ★

My father once explained to me that the "X" system of meas-
uring the diameter of tippet material derived from the primitive
method by which silkworm-gut tippets were made. A length of
gut was shaped and slenderized by drawing it through a small
round hole in a piece of metal. When the gut was pulled through
the aperture one time, it was labeled 1X. Drawing it through a
second time—2X—made it thinner, and so on.

My father's explanation was close to the truth, and satisfy-
ingly unscientific, but not quite accurate. In fact, the gut was
drawn through standardized apertures in metal plates used by
jewelers. Each jeweler's plate came with ten precisely-sized
holes, which stepped down in diameter from .010 (1X) to .001
(10X) in increments of .001 inch. Perversely, the bigger the X-
number, the smaller the hole.

This produces the "Rule of Eleven" for converting tippet X
size into diameter in thousanths of an inch: Subtract the X-
number from eleven. So 6X tippet has a diameter of .005 inch.

★ ★ ★

Probably because of many bad experiences with that early material, it took me a while to learn to trust skinny tippets. 4X was
about as light as I ever went, and even then, I felt a little show-
offy about it.

Several years ago, Harry Lane, who was guiding on the San
Juan River in New Mexico, straightened me out. He told me
that the best way to catch those muscular San Juan rainbows in
October, when I was there, was to drift tiny (size 22 and 24)
midge pupae on 6X tippets.

I opined that that was a pretty flimsy tippet for such big fish.

Harry grinned and took my rod. He tied three feet of 6X tippet (with a test weight of 3.5 pounds) to my leader and told me to hang onto the end of it. Then he stripped off a little line, backed up until the line and leader went taut, held the rod at a 45-degree angle, and said, "Okay, go ahead. Bust it."

I pulled and jerked and leaned my weight against the bend of the rod and the drag of the reel. I turned around and sprinted away. Harry "played" me expertly, and no matter how wildly I thrashed around, I could not break that tippet. I might not be as quick as a trout. But I'm bigger than most of them. It was an impressive exhibition of tippet strength, and since then I have felt confident fighting large fish aggressively on light tippets.

A lot has changed in the past 50-odd years. But I still think going down to 8X is an affectation.

13

From Bobs to Bugs

A LITTLE HISTORY

"Bass-bugging," wrote Ray Bergman, "is a type of fly-rod fishing that was born and raised right here in America. Considering that most fly fishing dates well back into English history, it's a young sport, young enough that as a boy [Bergman was born in 1891] I was among the first to fish these big bugs in this way."

Actually, bass-bug fishing is the oldest method of catching fish on hook and line in North America. In 1741, when William Bartram described how Florida's Seminole Indians fooled largemouth bass (which he called "trout") with a "bob", it's likely he was reporting on an angling method that had been practiced for generations before the Europeans invaded the continent.

"Two people are in a little canoe," wrote Bartram, "one sitting in the stern to steer, and the other near the bow, having a rod ten or twelve feet in length, to one end of which is tied a string line, about twenty inches in length, to which is fastened three large hooks, back to back. These are fixed very securely, and tied with the white hair of a deer's tail, shreds of a red garter, and some parti-colored feathers, all which form a tuft or tassel nearly as large as one's fist, and entirely cover and conceal the hooks; that are called a "bob." The steersman paddles softly, and proceeds slowly along shore; he now ingeniously swings the bob backwards and forwards, just above the surface and sometimes tips the water with it, when the unfortunate cheated trout [sic] instantly springs from under the reeds and seizes the exposed prey."

Today, when we cast our sleek spun-and-clipped deerhair bugs onto the water for bass, we are practicing an ancient and uniquely American technique that takes advantage of the bass's aggressive surface-feeding habits . . . and one that predates the use of cork and wood to float the lures. Modern fly-rod bass bugs—and the methods by which they are fished—are mere refinements of angling with the primitive bob.

Bass bugs have always been bass killers. It's doubtful if the Seminoles were much interested in sport or artfulness. They needed fish to eat, and Everglades largemouths were their most available species. So if bob fishing hadn't been an efficient way of capturing them, however much fun they had doing it, the Seminoles undoubtedly would've developed a deadlier method.

By the middle of the nineteenth century, bob fishing had expanded northwards into North Carolina, whose natives refined the lure into something that resembled a modern deerhair bug. Dr. James A. Henshall—whose *Book Of The Black Bass*, published in 1881, was the very first devoted to the subject of bass fishing—described his own experience with bobs:

"Happening to have a fish-hook in my pocket, I cut off a piece of the deer's tail, and made a 'bob.' Then, cutting a long, slender pole, and tying the bob to the end with a piece of strong twine some three feet long, we got into the boat, my comrade paddling and I manipulating the bob. . . .

"As my companion noiselessly paddled the boat along the fringe of rank grasses and luxuriant aquatic vegetation, I danced the bob along and over the water, now low, now high, and now dipping in the water—skimming, leaping and flying—till it seemed an uncanny thing. . . .

"Several bass rose to it, and swirled at it, until one more active than the rest grabbed it by a vicious lunge, and the hook was firmly in his jaw."

In *Flies* (1950), J. Edson Leonard explained how the North Carolina bob had evolved into something resembling a bass bug. Bobs were made, he reported, from squares of deerskin ("preferably from the skin from the shin bones"), which were cured, cut into strips "about the width of a shoe string," and soaked to make them pliable. "With the tail fastened on," wrote Leonard, "there remains only to tie the body in place and fasten on the wings. Taper one edge of the strip and tie it to the shank. Wind the strip around the shank, fasten it with the working silk, tie on the wings, and the bug will be complete. The hair will project nearly at right angles to the body and will weave back and forth when the bug is retrieved."

Whether Dr. Henshall actually invented the first bass bug made from spun and clipped deerhair, or whether the Henshall Bug was invented by somebody else and named after the father of American bass fishing, is uncertain. Leonard, for one, gives the doctor full credit. "Dr. James A. Henshall did more, perhaps, to exploit the first bass hair bugs than any other angler," Leonard wrote. "He is credited with having made the original hair bug, one which bears his name to this day." Others give the nod to Orley Tuttle, who concocted his Devil Bug in 1919.

I do not propose to resolve this mystery. Ray Bergman, who fished with bass bugs before 1919, is no help. He describes his childhood bugs as "big, beautiful artificials made of cork, feathers, and deerhair," but it's unclear whether any of them was the Henshall deerhair type, with no cork ingredients. The fact that Henshall never described anything that resembles what we now know as the Henshall Bug in his 1881 book suggests that, if he did invent it, it happened sometime later. But we do know that the good doctor fished with bobs. At least in retrospect, spinning deerhair seems to be such a logical next step and obvious improvement over winding a strip of hairy deerskin around a hook shank that it's easy to imagine Henshall, the consummate bass expert of his time, doing it. The Henshall Bug resembles a bob. It doesn't look anything like a Devil Bug.

The Henshall Bug features a tail of bucktail—white in the middle and a contrasting color on either side—flanked by splayed grizzly feathers. The body is built from flared and clipped natural deerhair, typically with a colorful stripe around its middle. The wings are fashioned from a bunch of bucktail tied in a downwing style over the clipped deerhair body and then divided and figure-eighted into position so that they stick out at right angles at the front of the hook. Most of our contemporary spun-and-clipped deerhair bugs are direct descendants of this design.

Orley Tuttle designed his bug to imitate the beetles he saw smallmouths eating on his local lake. He made it by laying a thick bunch of deerhair on top of the hook shank, lashing it down fore and aft, clipping the front into a stubby head, and leaving the rear tips of the hair to flare around the bend of the hook.

When Tuttle showed his odd creation to his wife, as the story goes, she declared: "Looks like the devil to me." And thus it was named the Devil Bug.

If the Devil Bug wasn't the first deerhair bass bug, it was certainly the first popular one. By 1922, Tuttle was selling 50,000 bugs a year in more than 800 combinations of color, size and design—moth bugs, beetle bugs, mouse bugs, and even a baby duck Devil Bug—and competing quite successfully with all the commercial cork-bodied bugs that had by that time hit the market. The Weber Life-Like Fly Company began mass producing Henshall Bugs sometime after that.

Both the Henshall Bug and the Devil Bug are easy enough to tie, and they'll still catch bass, although I don't know anyone who uses them anymore. This, I think, is too bad. You don't need to be a curmudgeonly old traditionalist to appreciate the uniquely American roots of bass-bug fishing and have the urge to revisit them now and then.

For that matter, given the pugnacious nature and unselective appetites of largemouth bass, I bet you could convince one to attack a bob.

★ ★ ★

Aside from a few pioneers who imitated Indian bob-fishing strategies, American fly fishermen relied on Old-World trout and salmon flies and techniques to catch bass well into the 20th century. For example, all of the so-called "bass flies" described and pictured in Mary Orvis Marbury's encyclopedic *Favorite Flies and Their Histories*, published in 1892, are simply larger and gaudier versions of the hackle-and-feather wet flies that Charles Cotton had written about two centuries earlier— or, for that matter, Dame Juliana before him. There is no evidence that non-native American anglers designed a single fly—topwater or subsurface—specifically for bass before 1910 or so.

Still, the effectiveness of surface-fishing for bass with a fly was well known. Those hackle-and-feather "bass flies" were typically fished on or near the surface. Dr. Henshall, in an 1880 magazine article, described the standard way to catch bass on flies: "The angler should endeavor to cast his flies as lightly as possible, causing them to settle as quietly as possible, and without a splash. After casting, the flies should be skipped along the surface in slightly curving lines, or by zigzag movements, occasionally allowing them to become submerged for several inches near likely-looking spots. If the current is swift, allow the flies to float naturally with it, at times, when they can be skittered back again, or withdrawn for a new cast."

Things changed dramatically shortly after the turn of the century when, as Paul Schullery wrote, ". . . the bass bug experienced a startling growth in popularity, and most of the enduring forms were created. There have been hundreds, perhaps even thousands, but they follow a few main types."

This sudden popularity resulted from two related factors. First, the effectiveness of high-floating cork bodies, in combination with feathers and other decorations, was discovered. Second, unlike feathers and hair, cork was a durable, easy-to-work-with material that lent itself to mass production.

In 1900 not a single commercially-made bass bug could be purchased. But by 1930, Schullery reports, "There was a bewildering assortment of bass bugs available, possibly even more than there are today." It wasn't so much that bass fishermen created a demand for commercially-manufactured fly-rod bugs. Rather, the production, distribution, and marketing of bass bugs created the sport of bass bugging. Designers such as Ernest Peckinpaugh and Cal McCarthy, manufacturers such as B. F. Wilder, and sporting writers such as Will H. Dilg worked together—and competed against each other—to popularize what had been a virtually unknown sport, and to create a burgeoning market for their products. By the early 1920s, what Jack Ellis calls the "Golden Age" of fly-fishing for bass had begun. And in those days, fly fishing for bass meant bass bugging.

Prototypes of the commercial cork-bodied bass bug had been used by the back-country "swampers" of Arkansas and Missouri, who lashed beer-bottle corks and turkey feathers to a hook and caught bass on them before the turn of the century. It's uncertain who deserves credit for the first true cork-bodied bass bug. Schullery gives the nod to William Jamison of Chicago, whose Coaxer (wide, flat cork body, red felt wings, and feather tail lying flat over the top of the hook) was created around 1910. A. J. McClane nominates Tennessean Ernest Peckinpaugh, whose Night Bug (feathers, bucktail, and a double hook, all lashed to a cork stopper) was manufactured by the John J. Hilderbrandt Company and popularized in sporting magazines by Will H. Dilg.

Jack Ellis contends that the first fly-rod popper was invented by none other than Theodore Gordon, but that fly-rod bassing was held in such low esteem among effete dry-fly anglers that to protect Gordon's shameful secret (he fished for bass!), he and his contemporaries deflected credit for inventing the lowly bass bug to Peckinpaugh.

We do know that by 1930, with considerable help from Dilg and the Hilderbrandt Company, Peckinpaugh had become the name most intimately associated with bass bugs. Dozens of variations of "Peck's Bugs" were made available in a highly competitive market.

Toward the end of his life, Peckinpaugh reflected on his first creation, the Night Bug. "I discovered that late in the afternoon," he wrote, "and at dusk, if I could keep a bucktail fly on top of the water, I would catch more fish. This gave me the idea of putting a cork on a hook, and tying the bucktail hair to the lure, and in that way making it stay on the surface. A little experimenting quickly showed me that a single hook could not be securely fastened to the cork, but I did find that by using a double hook, I could make a very solid bug. Therefore, all the first bass bugs I made were on double hooks. These bugs were designed for taking bream. I found that just before dark the bream would strike on the surface and I could catch them by using one of these little cork body bugs.

"There was practically no further development in these bugs until 1910 or 1911. I am uncertain about which year. Anyway, at this particular time, my work as a contractor kept me pretty busy and the jobs were always so far away from home that they interfered considerably with my usual periods of fishing. By the time I arrived at one of the lakes or ponds where I usually fished, it would be just about dark, so I was compelled to fish at night. I then discovered that bass would strike the same bugs which I had been using for bream. But the hook was small and I lost most of the fish. This inspired me to make a larger edition of the double hook bugs, and inasmuch as they were developed for night fishing, I called them 'Night Bugs.' I made these bass bugs in many colors of feathers and bucktail hair."

When the Great War broke out in Europe in 1914, Peckinpaugh lost his British source of double hooks and was forced to adapt his Night Bug to the single hook. He tied for friends and sold them locally in Chattanooga. Bass-fishing tourists bought them, and thus Peckinpaugh's bugs migrated to other parts of the country and eventually to the businessmen who would make them for the market.

Other popular cork-bodied bugs of the 1920s and '30's were the Cal-Mac moth, a flat-winged affair devised by Cal McCarthy, and the Wilder-Dilg, the prototype for the still-popular "feathered minnow" or Sneaky Pete, which featured a pointed nose, bullet-shaped body, wound hackle at the butt, and a long tail of hackle feathers.

Around this time, Tom Loving of Baltimore invented his Gerbubble Bug, which Joe Brooks called "the best largemouth bug I've ever used." Loving's creation featured hackle feathers inserted into slits cut along both sides of the cork body so that the fibers stuck out perpendicular to the hook shank, creating the effect of dozens of legs kicking at the water's surface.

Meanwhile, fly tiers were creating their own deerhair counterparts of the commercial cork-bodied bugs. Orley Tuttle's popular Devil Bug and the spun-and-clipped deerhair Henshall Bug sparked the creativity of a generation of clever fly tiers such as Joe Messenger, who elevated the tying of deerhair bugs to an art form in the 1930s. Messenger crafted his realistic and utterly elegant frogs by stacking rather than spinning the deerhair body. This technique involved holding a bundle of hair in place to prevent it from twirling 360 degrees around the shank of the hook as he drew the thread tight over it to make it flare. In this way, Messenger created two-toned clipped deerhair frogs with pale bellies and green backs. To make protruding, kicking legs, he inserted a piece of wire into a bunch of two-tone bucktail, wound over the knees with thread, bent the wire into shape, and fixed the joints with glue.

By 1940 or so, bass bugs had become as integral to fly fishing as dry flies. Fly-fishing or fly-tying books were considered incomplete if they failed to include a section on bugs. Even a book as general and concise as H. G. Tapply's *Tackle Tinkering* (1945), which covered baitcasting and live-bait methods as well as fly fishing, included detailed instructions on making both cork-bodied and spun-deerhair bugs.

William Bayard Sturgis (*Fly-Tying*, 1940) and William F. Blades (*Fishing Flies And Fly Tying*, 1951), probably the most innovative and influential tiers of their era, continued to expand the art of bass-bug making. Both Sturgis and Blades gave the same attention to hair- and cork-bodied bugs as they did to trout and salmon flies. Their hair mice, frogs, crawfish, moths, and cork poppers were logical extensions of the art of bug-making.

In 1947, Joe Brooks published *Bass Bug Fishing*, the first book devoted exclusively to that subject. Finally, it seemed, fly fishermen had fully embraced bass as quarry that deserved as much respect as trout and salmon, and fishermen in general accepted the fly rod as a deadly weapon for catching bass.

Then everything changed.

★ ★ ★

Spinning landed in North America shortly after World War II. It democratized fishing almost overnight. With spinning gear, anyone could make a long, smooth cast on his first try, with none of those backlashes that plagued level-wind baitcasters or any of that awkward back-and-forth flailing around that frustrated the beginning fly caster.

Spinning gave fishing to the people, and bass, particularly largemouths, were the people's fish. By the middle of this century, both largemouths and smallmouths had migrated to every state in the lower 48. Almost every body of fresh water held bass. If it didn't, somebody transplanted them. Bass were accessible and abundant, and they grew big. They were aggressive and impetuous, unlike the moody trout. Bass were blue-collar fish; trout were high-society. In a bar-room brawl, you'd put your money on any bass over the toughest trout in the joint.

It's entirely consistent with the American spirit that bass fishing would become a competitive sport and a big business. The Bass Anglers Sportsman Society (B.A.S.S.) was founded in the 1960s, and soon Jimmy Houston and Roland Martin and Bill Dance became household names. Industries competed with each other to invent artificial lures that bass would eat. Bass lures were called "baits," and they had down-to-earth designations—"plastic worms" and "jig-and-pigs," "stickbaits" and "buzzbaits," "spinnerbaits" and "crankbaits." They were made of rubber and plastic and metal, and they came in myriad colors, many of which could be found nowhere in nature, but which, their creators claimed, drove bass nuts. They all worked, of course. Bass eat anything. But an endorsement from a bass champion guaranteed big sales.

Other enterprising businessmen designed boats and motors and electronics specifically for bass fishermen. They adapted space-age materials to the construction of lines, rods and reels, and addicted bassmen bought that stuff, too.

With money on the line, competitive bass fishermen began to study the habits of their quarry and the ways that bass behavior correlated with season and weather and water temperature and other variables. They studied the habits and behavior of bass prey, too, so that they could imitate them with the shape, color, size, and action of their lures. They made a science of bass fishing. And they sure could catch 'em.

Tournament bass fishing quickly spread north and west until, by the late 70s or so, bass clubs were sponsoring contests all over the country. Recreational, non-competitive bass fishing, or course, mirrored the exploding popularity of the tournaments. For every competitive pro, there were hundreds of amateurs who trailered boats, hunted bass obsessively with fishfinders and spinning rods, and dreamed of joining the tournament circuit.

The arrival of spinning in the 1940s inevitably produced a decline in the popularity of fly fishing in general, and in fly fishing for bass in particular. Jack Ellis calls the first three post-war decades "The Dark Age" of fly-rod bass-bug fishing. Throwing bugs from a clunky old rowboat, compared to the new high-tech methods, struck with-it anglers of that era as old-fashioned, ineffective, and vaguely amusing. Typical of the new attitude was that of outdoor scribe Jason Lucas, who wrote in 1947: "Bass bugging is an extremely crude form of fly fishing, if fly fishing it can be called . . . A child of average mentality should learn bass bugging in a few minutes." Bass fishing, under the influence of Lucas and many others, was becoming a science for spin- and baitcasters, and while it wasn't to become apparent until sometime in the 1970s, the bass-boat/high-tech/big-money tournament revolution had begun.

The commercial market for deerhair bass bugs dried up during the post-war years, but a few diehards continued to fool around at the vise. Roy Yates created a deerhair version of the Wilder-Dilg feathered minnow—a design he adapted from Don Gapen's Muddler, and which he called The Deacon. A few years later, H. G. Tapply created his higher-floating, noisier, all-deerhair version of The Deacon. He never got around to giving it a name, so, by default, it came to be called Tap's Bug.

Hard-bodied fly-rod bugs continued to be manufactured, and new materials such as foam and molded plastic were introduced. But the designs didn't change, as lure manufacturers' creative energies shifted to "baits" that could be cast with spinning and baitcasting outfits. That particular market was exploding.

The pleasures of top-water fly-rodding for bass continued to be chronicled in books and magazines through the '50s, '60s, and '70s by that era's most respected fishing writers, notably Joe Brooks, John Alden Knight, A. J. McClane, Harold F. Blaisdell, Tom Nixon, Ray Bergman, H. G. Tapply, Charles Waterman, and Tom McNally. All of these esteemed angling gurus wrote fondly of fly-rod bass-bug fishing, but only Nixon fished for bass exclusively with the fly rod, and Brooks' book was the only one that focused exclusively on bass-bugging. The other writers all fished widely, for a variety of species, and with whatever tackle promised success. You could catch bass on the fly rod, they insisted. But you could catch them other ways, too. As Bergman lamented, there seemed to be a "growing apathy toward fly fishing on the part of bass anglers."

So in the "Dark Age" of the post-war high-tech revolution, bass bugging became a novelty in the popular mind, a harmless (and "crude") sport that was being kept alive by nostalgic old-timers who'd sometimes rather flail around with fly rods than catch a lot of bass.

★ ★ ★

The revival of bass-bug fishing—what Nick Lyons has called "the bass-fly revolution"—began in the 1970s and can be credited largely to the efforts of Dave Whitlock who, in Jack Ellis's words, "made bass bugging respectable." Whitlock, says Ellis, "brought dignity, artistry, and class to bass bugging. He was the first famous bass bugger (there's got to be a better term) in history who did not, with the lone exception of Messinger, occasionally use the casting rod."

Whitlock's bass-fly designs—subsurface as well as topwater—are colorful, sleek, and imitative, and he writes about fly-rod bassing with knowledgeable enthusiasm. "Fly fishing for bass," he says, "may well be the most exciting, pleasurable, and consistently rewarding method of fishing that exists today in North America. . . . Bass are terrific fun on a fly rod!"

Whitlock devised bass flies and developed fly-fishing techniques, he says, by "studying and adapting the successful methods of the saltwater fly fishers and the spin and baitcasting bass fishermen." His flies are complicated and eye-catching—to the angler, certainly, and probably to bass as well. They imitate not only natural bass prey, but also the lures that spin-fishermen cast in their tournaments.

Those who contend that it's the wiggle, glug and burble that makes bass gobble flies might feel that Whitlock dresses his bass flies with unnecessary and redundant appendages and decorations. His Whit Hair-Bug Series, for example, are basic Tap's bugs in a variety of color combinations, complete with eyes, multi-material tails, glitter, and rubber legs. Whether Whitlock's elegant creations catch more bass than simpler, less imitative flies is debatable, but they surely have served the purpose of convincing an ever-widening population of anglers to take up fly-fishing for bass. His various deerhair divers, underwater swimmers, bottom flies and jigs look and behave even more like actual bass prey than their metal and plastic counterparts favored by the tournament bassmen.

Whitlock's imitative hair-and-feather bass flies—along with his enthusiastic promotion of fly fishing for bass—have converted a generation of trout anglers, who are predisposed to the concept of imitation, to the fun of fly-rod bass fishing. His bugs and lures offer fly fishermen lifelike imitations of all known bass prey—and valid options to virtually every lure the tournament bassers can throw with a spinning or baitcasting rod. For every stickbait and crankbait and jig and rubber worm, there is a corresponding Whitlock creation for the fly fisherman—the Whit Hair Bug, Mouserat, Wigglelegs Frog, Snakey, Eeelworm Streamer, Hare Water Pup, Chamois Spring Lizard, Haregrub, Water Snake, Golden Shiner, Water Dog, Sand Eel, Deerhair Gerbubble Bug . . . the list goes on.

Other contemporary bass-fly inventors and practitioners such as Larry Dahlberg, best known for his innovative deerhair diver, John Betts, Bob Clouser, Dick Stewart, A. D. Livingston, Harry Murray, Jack Ellis, C. Boyd Pfeiffer, and Jack Gartside have made important contributions to the Whitlock bass-fly revival. Iconic angling writers like Nick Lyons and John Gierach chronicle the simple, poetic joys of fly-rod bugging. We probably don't really need an arsenal of imitative flies to catch bass but, for the sake of the sport of fly-rod bassing, I'm glad we have them. Their variety gives us genuine respectability, the inspiration to experiment at the vise and on the water, and, when the fishing is slow, legitimate options to old-fashioned hair and cork bugs.

But, on a soft summer evening, I'm usually quite content to tie on something not much different from a strip-skin bob—a Henshall Bug, maybe, or a yellow Tap's Bug. I'll plop it near a fallen tree, watch the rings widen and dissipate before making it go *ker-PLOOP*, and wait for that sudden implosion of water. It reminds me that I am not that far removed from the Seminole Indians of the 17th century. I think it's good for my soul to stay in touch with my roots.

14

Harm's Way

L ast summer I was chucking a floating damselfly imitation at some cruising brown trout on a Montana pond when, in the midst of a double-haul, my 4-weight sort of collapsed. When I stripped in my line, I saw that a foot of graphite rod tip had slithered down the line and gotten tangled with the fly.

The next day, drifting weighted stonefly nymphs on the Yellowstone, I hooked a medium-sized rainbow and my back-up 4-weight snapped.

Two broken rods in two days. For the rest of the trip I had to use my back-up-back-up 3-weight, which was not designed to cast weighted stonefly nymphs and conehead bunny streamers in the Montana wind.

When I got home I called the manufacturer of the two broken rods (both came from the same maker). I had a tale of woe all prepared. It wasn't my fault. I wasn't doing anything wrong. I love my rods and always treat them like the very expensive pieces of fine-tuned machinery they are.

The woman on the other end of the line listened without comment and then asked for the rods' serial numbers and my address. Two weeks later I had replacements for both rods, no charge, no questions asked.

I'm not complaining, but truthfully, it didn't seem right. I was brought up to accept responsibility for what I did. If you broke a rod, you fixed it. A rod with a shortened tip never quite casts the same, of course. But you made do.

I started fishing when fly rods were all made from split bamboo. I broke a lot of rods when I was a kid. Screen doors and car doors slammed on them. They got stepped on and stubbed in the ground and caught in bicycle spokes. I always felt bad, but my father would just say, "Things break," just like, when I was playing shortstop and bobbled a grounder, he'd say, "Errors are part of the game."

One June afternoon Dad and I were trolling for rainbows on Walden Pond with his friend Lenox Putnam. Put was in the bow, Dad ran the motor from the stern, and I had the middle seat. We'd piled quite a lot of equipment into our little boat, and once we got underway Dad said, "Let's get some of this stuff stowed out of harm's way."

Put laughed, leaned forward, and tapped my shoulder. "Hello, there, Harm," he said.

Dad thought that was pretty funny, and for several years thereafter I was known among my father's fishing companions as Harm.

★ ★ ★

My first fly rod was an 8½-foot 3-piece Montague, complete with cloth sleeve and aluminum tube, a Christmas present when I was ten. I know now that it was a cheap, mass-produced stick, but I thought it was gorgeous. I spent the next four months setting it up and waving it around and running my fingertips over its smooth varnished finish.

At sunrise on the third Saturday of the following April, I was sprinting down the sloping path to my Opening Day trout pond with my brand-new Montague, all strung up with an Eagle Claw hook and a cork-stopper bobber in one hand and a can of freshly-dug worms in the other, when a tree branch reached out, snagged my rod, and splintered the tip section.

Instead of crying, my first impulse, I disjointed the broken tip, and when I got to the pond, I used the butt and middle sections of my new Montague to muscle my baited hook into the water. Caught a couple of pale hatchery brookies, too.

When I got home, I had to tell my father that I'd broken my new rod before I ever got to fish with it. He seemed more pleased with the fact that I'd improvised with two-thirds of a rod than upset that I'd busted it.

Then he told me how it worked: "You break it, you fix it."

And so I learned how to splice and glue and wrap splintered bamboo, how to space and attach running guides and tiptops, how to steel-wool, burnish and revarnish the finish.

I'd like to report that I also learned not to run in the woods carrying a strung-up fly rod. But the fact is, Harm has been breaking things all his life.

★ ★ ★

I grew up in a time—or at least in a household—where you took responsibility for your gear, and in a nostalgic, irrational sort of way, I sometimes think of that time as the Good Old Days.

115

Compared to today, our equipment was clunky. Waders were made of heavy canvas. When they sprang leaks, you used a flashlight in a dark room to find the holes and then you patched them with a bicycle-tube repair kit. You hung them upside down to dry (you could make a good wader-hanger by bending a pair of coathangers and nailing them to the wall) so they wouldn't rot.

The early nylon fly lines got tacky and kinky if you didn't strip them out onto a newspaper to dry after every day of fishing. If the line's finish cracked, you soaked it in a 50-50 mixture of boiled linseed oil and spar varnish. You had to be able to splice sections of line together and whip loops onto the ends to keep them serviceable year after year. It would never occur to you to throw away an old fly line.

I learned how to mix my own insect repellent (a mixture of citronella, oil of cedar, camphor, pennyroyal oil, petroleum jelly, and pine tar) and dry-fly floatant (paraffin dissolved in lighter fluid). Mineral oil made a good fly-line dressing. I learned leader formulas and knots, because they hadn't yet invented knotless tapered leaders.

I learned how to take apart, clean, and oil my reels. I sharpened my hooks, polished my spinners and spoons, and made my own sinkers (pour molten lead into holes you've gouged into the flat side of half a potato). I had dozens of uses for paperclips, safety pins, and bobby pins.

I tied my own flies because the only place I could buy them was the hardware store, which stocked only snelled wet flies. Mail-order and on-line options didn't exist. As far as I knew, Stoddards in Boston was the only store in Massachusetts that

sold a legitimate assortment of flies, and it took half a day riding
a bus and then a train to get there, even if I had some money. So
I scavenged road kill (woodchuck, squirrel and raccoon, mainly)
for their hair. I saved all the feathers from the pheasants, woodcock, grouse and ducks that I shot, and I snuck over to Bob
Allen's chicken coop next door and plucked feathers from his
rooster's neck. I learned how to dye bucktails and feathers. I
filched yarn and scraps of wool from my mother's knitting
basket. I made flash from Christmas tree tinsel and aluminum
foil. I tied flies from the materials I had, and if I didn't have some
ingredient I needed, I used something else.

Like rod and wader repairing and caring for equipment and
making the stuff you couldn't buy, fly tying was an essential skill
for a fly fisherman back then. Being an angler involved a lot of
time-consuming and fussy work. I don't remember getting any
particular sense of satisfaction from doing it all myself. That's just
the Way It Was.

I love breathable waders and tapered knotless leaders and the
myriad fly-tying materials and the wonderfully useful doodads
you can buy with a credit card and a few clicks of a mouse these
days. I'm certainly not complaining about full-replacement-no-
questions-asked rod warranties, either.

Whenever I'm tempted to wax nostalgic about the Good
Old Days, as I increasingly am, I remind myself that back then
cesspools spewed domestic sewage directly into the Upper
Connecticut River, festooning the bushes along the banks with
strips of toilet paper. Effluent from textile factories ran the
Nashua River bright red or green or purple, depending on
what day of the week it was. In those days a creel or a fish

stringer was essential equipment. Nobody practiced catch and release. There was no such thing as sunscreen, although skin cancer had already been invented. There were no magazines devoted to fly fishing, never mind Saturday-morning cable TV shows or instructional videos.

My father wrote books and magazine articles about how to make and fix and improvise stuff for fishing. But he was above all else a Yankee pragmatist. He believed in progress. He liked to say, "These right here are the Good Old Days." He embraced the new carefree fly lines and knotless leaders and breathable waders, and he was happy to buy bug dope and dry-fly repellent that worked way better than the concoctions he made. He reminded me that the trout fishing on the Upper Connecticut had never been better, and that largemouth bass were thriving in the once-dead Nashua.

When fiberglass came along, my father simply stopped using bamboo rods. "Fiberglass rods are lighter and cast better," he said, and, with an elbow nudge to my ribs, he added, "and they're practically unbreakable, so you don't have to keep them out of Harm's way."

15

Toy Rods

When you go striper or steelhead fishing with Fred Jennings, the first thing you notice is that he catches way more fish, and bigger fish, than you do. If you watch him closely, you see that he casts farther than you do, with less false casting and with less apparent effort in general, even in the wind, and he muscles his fish in more efficiently and releases them more quickly than you do.

Then you notice his fly rod. It's a six-foot, two-weight wand. A mere toy. And you wonder what this man is trying to prove.

He's happy to talk about it.

WGT: Everybody knows that you need a long, stiff rod to fight big fish and bring them in before they—and you—are utterly exhausted. You seem to do fine—okay, you do great—with your baby rod, but couldn't you fight and land your fish even better with a man-sized rod?

FJ: It seems to be an unquestioned assumption that the use of light tackle kills fish because one must baby them far too much. This is something I *know* to be wrong. The myth that one needs long stiff rods and heavy lines for big fish has been very destructive.

WGT: Huh? A myth? Destructive?

FJ: What people don't seem to realize when they denigrate my use of light tackle because it "kills the fish" by playing them too long is that I land my fish faster than almost anyone else I fish with. What determines how hard you can pull on a fish has *absolutely nothing* to do with the weight of the line that you are hurling into the air. It has to do with tippet strength and the design of the rod.

WGT: So this short-rod stuff isn't some romantic affectation?

FJ: No. It's physics. When my 6-foot 2-weight rod is bent hard into a fish, for a given torque at my wrist (in foot-pounds), more than half of that goes to the line tension, because the "effective length" of my rod when bent that way is somewhat less than two feet. So for 20 foot-pounds, I am putting more than 10 pounds of tension on the line itself where it comes out of the rod tip going out to the fish. With the friction of the water, that is all one would ever want to exert, at least on a 15-pound tippet and a crashing fish, and that's living dangerously. Understand?

WGT: Well, sort of. You're saying a short rod is *more* efficient than a long one?

FJ: Absolutely. Consider the same situation with a 9 foot 8-weight rod. Here, an exertion of 20 foot-pounds at the lower end of the rod involves about 7 feet of rod in terms of "effective length" once bent, which yields less than one-third the tension at the rod tip on the line, namely just under 3 pounds of tension. So, to pull 10 pounds of tension at the rod tip (assuming 3 feet is lost to the bend with this heavier pull), one must exert 60 foot-pounds of torque at the handle instead of only 20. When I am fighting a very large fish, I pull as hard as my hand and arm strength allow, often with the reel braced against my forearm or my midriff. I am getting more tension for the amount of effort expended than someone with a long stiff rod. This means that I can bring a fish in faster due to better leverage than anyone with a long rod.

WGT: I'm not sure I followed all that, but it sounds impressive. It's all about leverage, huh?

FJ: Leverage is a big part of it, sure. But when it comes to fighting big fish, the real advantage of a light short rod is its incredible sensitivity. You can feel every move a fish makes during a fight, and most especially on a big fish. You can feel what the fish is doing. You can tell when it's about to run, and you can anticipate it and stop it by putting on some pressure at those moments. The big sticks don't have anywhere near the sensitivity of my short light rods, nor are they anywhere near as much fun to fight a fish on.

WGT: I've seen how efficiently you land and release your fish after you get them in. You want me to believe the short rod helps here, too?

FJ: You bet. When landing a fish with the longer rods, you have almost no control of that fish. If you can use a net or a gaff and you tire the fish out enough, then you can control it because it's exhausted. But the fish I bring in on my short rods are still green and agile when I release them.

WGT: There must be some technique to it.

FJ: Right. With a short rod, I bring in the line until I have only about two feet or less of leader left outside the rod tip, and then even a pretty wild fish can be controlled very well. The thing to remember is to extend your rod hand all the way out from your body. Otherwise you will "candy-cane" the rod and break it. That position allows you to bend the length of the short rod over your head, so the fish comes in on the other side of you under tight control. From here, run your hand down the leader either to the fly or to the lower jaw of the fish. Grabbing the line on big fish is a great mistake and will often cost you a fly.

WGT: Okay, but surely your baby rod seriously handicaps your casting. You don't look that strong . . .

FJ: You're right. My arms aren't very strong. That's precisely why I like short rods. They're much easier to cast without getting tired. A very short rod gives you much higher line speed. The advantage is that you can use a lighter line in the wind and it moves faster through the air than it does with a longer rod. Short light rods cannot be powered through a cast. You need to use timing and grace, not power. I'm always surprised at how many people used to big long rods simply cannot cast at all with my short light ones. They try to power the rod and that just doesn't work.

WGT: I have to admit that you seem to cast farther with your little wand than I do with my man-sized rod.

FJ: I am always surprised when I fish with people using long heavy rods and find that I am casting about 10–20 feet farther than they are. I would agree, however, that you can cast farther with long rods than you can with shorter ones *if you don't have much skill*. The long rods are slower so the timing is not as critical. But, once you learn how to cast a light short rod, it is so much easier that, when you go back to the big rod, it just feels like a club.

WGT: Hm. Skill, huh?

FJ: I didn't necessarily mean you. But if the shoe fits.

WGT: What about casting in the wind? Surely your flimsy little stick handicaps you there?

FJ: Au contraire. Casting into wind with long rods and heavy, fat-diameter lines puts more stress on your arm and requires more work. The longer the rod, the more slowly the line moves through the air, and heavy lines are more wind resistant. To beat a stiff wind, go short and use light lines. Also, when you cast short rods in the wind, the line is down nearer the water where the wind doesn't blow as hard.

WGT: I notice you use a shooting head. How important is the way you rig up?

FJ: After a lot of trial and error, I've developed a rig that works beautifully with my short, light rods. I use a 30-foot shooting head, flat mono running line, and a ten-foot fifteen-pound leader for stripers. I usually fish with weighted flies like Clousers. There are many advantages to this rig. The flat mono shoots like a dream When I get to the flyline in my retrieve I know it's time to pick up and cast, and when I'm on my game I can throw a cast with only one false-cast, thus keeping my fly in the water for a maximum amount of time. Another nice feature of this rig is that it maximizes the amount of backing I can wind onto the small reels that balance the little rods.

WGT: Thanks for sharing your secrets.

FJ: I don't have any secrets. I want people to understand. I'd like to debunk the conventional wisdom about big rods being better and more sportsmanlike. I really believe that folks will have more fun—and catch more fish—using short, light rods. This prejudice against these rods deprives anglers of a great deal of pleasure. I've seen the delight people get from fighting big fish on light rods again and again when I've put one of my outfits in their hands.

PART IV

Fly Fishing
Here and There

"There is no use in your walking five miles to fish when you can depend on being just as unsuccessful near home."
—Mark Twain

"The wildness and adventure that are in fishing still recommend it to me."
—Henry David Thoreau, *Walden*

"I fish all the time when I'm at home; so when I get a chance to go on vacation, I make sure I get in plenty of fishing."
—Thomas McGuane, *An Outside Chance*

16

Porcupine Brook

I happened upon Porcupine Brook while exploring some promising woodcock cover last October. Burt, my Brittany, had wandered off, as he often does, and when I could no longer hear his bell, and he refused to come when I yelled at him, I had to go looking for him.

I found him stretched out on point in an alder thicket on the other side of a little winding brook. When I jumped across so I could kick up Burt's woodcock, several quick shadows darted across the sandy bottom.

I missed the woodcock, of course. A little farther along Burt pointed again, and I missed again, which is how he and I generally do it. No matter. It looked like we'd found ourselves a nice woodcock cover.

We followed that string of alders along the boggy upstream course of the brook. It was good-looking cover, and Burt hunted it well. But the brook kept distracting me. It snaked through some swamp, curved around the edge of a meadow, and eventually dissipated in a hillside that was wet with springholes. It ran slow, narrow, and deep in most places, with dark undercuts, rock-rimmed pools, a few quick riffles. Willows and alders grew thick along its banks, and a lot of old blowdown deflected the current and gouged out deep holes. It was a typical New England woodland brook. In most places I could jump across it. In a few places it widened to ten or twelve feet.

When I got home, I took out my topographic map and drew a red circle around my new woodcock cover. The thin snaky blue line that wandered through it was labeled Porcupine Brook. It eventually ran into a larger stream, and that stream emptied into a river that joined up with another river and on to the sea.

I remembered those quick shadows I'd seen panicking over the sand bottom and thought, hopefully: Wild New England brook trout.

The Hillsborough county trout-stocking records did not list Porcupine Brook. However, the stream it ran into, and the river that stream emptied into, were both stocked. So those shadows probably weren't pure natives, uncontaminated with hatchery genes. But I figured I'd spotted some wild trout, fish that had had been born right there in Porcupine Brook, and I promised myself that come spring I'd explore my new woodcock cover with a rod instead of a shotgun.

★ ★ ★

Porcupine Brook reminded me of the little brook that my father and I fished ritually every Patriot's Day, April 19, which was a state holiday in Massachusetts, when I was a kid. When Dad and I talked about it, we called it Trout Brook, secure in the knowledge that anybody who overheard us would never find it by that name on any map. Dad had stumbled upon Trout Brook during the woodcock season, the same way I found Porcupine Brook.

We parked on a dirt road and intercepted Trout Brook deep in a swamp after a twenty-minute trek through the woods. Then we leap-frogged each other, alternating pools, working our way downstream to where the brook passed under the road near where we'd left the car. Like Porcupine Brook, Trout Brook ran slow and narrow and dark, and its brushy banks precluded any kind of casting. So we dug some worms, impaled one just once (to give it plenty of wiggle) on a Size 10 wet-fly hook, pinched a single small split-shot six inches up the tippet, and steered it through the likely-looking trout holes with a fly rod.

We didn't wade. We slogged along the muddy banks and poked the rod through the openings in the bushes. We worked mostly from our knees, because the trout that lived there were plenty spooky. It took a lot of concentration to detect a bite. The leader would hesitate or twitch, or you might just sense something vibrating up the fly line to your fingers.

Dad believed that the brookies we caught on Patriot's Day were pure natives. Maybe, maybe not. But they were certainly wild fish. Their spots glowed like drops of fresh blood and their olive backs were sharply vermiculated. They were slim, but not skinny, and they felt muscular in your hand. They mostly ran from finger-sized to six or seven inches. We always kept half a dozen six-inchers for supper and threw back those that were smaller or significantly larger. Once I derricked in a fish from Trout Brook that measured eleven inches. Dad proclaimed that one a monster, and we returned it carefully so that it might pass its monster genes on to new generations.

Alas, one Patriot's Day we found orange surveyor's stakes scattered through the woods and along the banks of Trout Brook, and a year later the forest had been clearcut and the hills bulldozed level. The brook ran warm and dirty through a straight muddy ditch.

★ ★ ★

The April after Burt and I stumbled upon Porcupine Brook, I went back. I suppose I was trying to relive some old and happy memories of fishing with my father when I was a kid. I also wanted to learn what manner of fish lived in this brook. But mainly, I just felt like going fishing on a nice April afternoon.

I brought an old 7½-foot fiberglass fly rod, a 4-weight forward-tapered floating line with a seven-foot leader, a spool of 4X tippet, some Size 10 wet-fly hooks, a few split shots, and a Zip-Loc bag full of freshly-dug worms.

I hadn't fished with worms for many years. When I was growing up, I fished every way that I could for every species of fish that lived, but I had the most faith in worms. No freshwater fish would pass up a worm, but you had to put it where the fish was living in a manner that appeared natural, and that took skill and knowledge. Fishing a trout brook with a worm demanded a stealthy approach, an accurate reading of the water, and a careful presentation of the bait. It had to tumble along with the currents at the right depth. I didn't know the term "drag," but I learned all about it by drifting worms in trout brooks. The fish told you when you'd done everything right.

My only rod back then was a clunky three-piece 8½ foot Montague made from split bamboo. I learned the feel of a fly rod by lobbing and roll-casting baited hooks. Casting flies came easily and naturally to me after doing that.

I caught a several pretty little brookies from Porcupine Brook that April day, working my way downstream from pool to pool the way Dad and I did it fifty years ago. I got muddy and scratched and bitten by bugs. It was a wonderful afternoon of fishing. It reminded me of where I'd come from and how I'd gotten to where I am.

A few days later I told one of my fly-fishing buddies about it.

"You didn't keep any fish?" he said.

I nodded. "Put 'em all back."

"But didn't they swallow the hook?"

"Nope. I debarbed it and tightened on the fish as soon as they hit the worm, just the way you do with nymphs. They were all lip-hooked."

"You used a fly rod, though, eh?"

I nodded.

"But you didn't try casting flies?"

"You can't cast on Porcupine Brook. Impossible. Too narrow and brushy."

"So you used your fly rod just to steer your, um, your *bait* into the holes." He pronounced the word "bait" as if he were naming a disgusting waste product.

"Exactly."

"Hm," he said. "So tell me. Why didn't you use nymphs? I mean, a caddis pupa or even a San Juan worm . . ."

"I suppose I could have," I said, "but what's the difference?"

He frowned for a minute. Then he said, "Well, at least you would've been fly fishing."

★ ★ ★

The fly-fishing snob was famously lampooned on the cover of the Spring 1933 L. L. Bean catalog in a painting which depicted a barefoot boy with a sapling for a rod showing a string of trout to a portly gentleman with a fly rod under his arm. The portly gentleman—he's smoking a pipe and wearing a bow tie—is glancing around furtively and reaching for his wallet.

H. T. Webster responded to this clichéd scenario in a 1940 cartoon that appeared in the *New York Herald Tribune*. Webster shows a smug even-more-portly gentleman holding a fly rod with half a dozen fat trout laid out on the stream bank and a barefoot boy gazing longingly down at the fish. In case the message wasn't clear, the gentleman is saying, "Hm. You look like th' boy in th' illustrated calendars who always sells his string of trout to th' old fisherman. Better take a couple of mine—I'd hate to see a nice youngster like you go home skunked." And to drive home the point, the cartoon's caption reads: "The fisherman with expensive tackle who is invariably humiliated by the boy with the hickory pole and a bent pin, finally comes through."

Nowadays, the downfall of the fly-fishing purist is not that he might be outfished by a barefoot boy with a hickory pole and a can of worms. It's that he'll never spend an April afternoon catching wild six-inch brookies from Porcupine Brook.

17

The Natives of Minipi

From the window of our Twin Otter in the summer of 2004, the watery tundra of Labrador looked exactly the way it did from the window of Lee Wulff's Super Cub in 1957—which was exactly the way it has looked since the glaciers retreated 20,000 years ago. It's all flat and green and wet. No roads. No dwellings. Just 115,000 square miles of nothing but lakes and rivers, many of them nameless, and bogs and rocks and scraggly spruce forest and moss, from horizon to horizon.

From 1000 feet, the lakes of the Minipi watershed got Wulff's attention. They are shallow—no more than 6 to 12 feet deep in most places—so the sunlight penetrates to the bottom, making them incredibly fertile. In the brief Labrador growing season (mid-June through early September) the Minipi system is a nursery for oversized mayflies—brown and green drakes and *hexagenia* in sizes 6 to 10—and for the biggest, healthiest, purest strain of wild native brook trout in the world.

Put the two together—brookies up to nine pounds sipping big duns and spinners (and any reasonable imitation tied to a 2X tippet) off a flat lake surface—and you've got a unique and precious resource and a fly-fishing experience that Wulff called "the greatest brook trout fishing in North America."

It's as good today as it was in 1957. I have fished there twice in the past decade, a total of twelve full days and evenings. Both times the guides were complaining about the spotty hatches and the slow fishing. I landed an average of slightly more than two brook trout-of-a-lifetime per day, all but one of which weighed over four pounds (Minipi fish are weighed, not measured). My biggest, a 7¾-pounder, inhaled a deerhair mouse (the guides call it a "moose"). Most of the fish I caught had been spotted gulping drake duns and spinners, and they sucked my big dry flies off the flat lake surface with unforgettable kissing sounds.

Slow fishing? Compared to what? I'm not sure I'd want to catch more than two trophy brook trout a day although, according to the three camps' meticulously-kept log books, their guests do it routinely.

One of my partners, Steven Cooper, released a brookie that weighed 8½ pounds. Elliot Schildkrout, fishing from the same boat on the same day, landed an 8-pounder. Both fish ate dry flies.

★ ★ ★

When he realized what he had discovered, Wulff lobbied the Canadian and provincial governments to protect the Minipi waters with special regulations. "A trout is too valuable to be caught only once," he famously said, "and that goes double for the giant brookies of Minipi."

The governments responded by granting an exclusive license for outfitting the Minipi watershed to Wulff's friend, local guide Ray Cooper. In 1967 Wulff helped Cooper set up a fly-in camp on White Lake, which Cooper renamed Anne Marie after his daughter. In 1979 Cooper sold the operation to Jack and Lorraine Cooper (no relation), who have run it ever since. The Coopers built another camp on Lake Minonopi, at the headwaters of the watershed, and a bigger lodge on Lake Minipi. All three facilities are accessible only by float plane. From these outposts, for the brief Labrador trout-fishing season, come all of the angling pressure on the Minipi brookies: About 100 anglers a year catching and releasing fish on single barbless hooks from 250 square miles of lakes and rivers.

The Coopers allow each fisherman to keep one trophy trout per week, presumably for mounting. The guides told me that they don't remember the last time anybody actually killed a trout. It would be tolerated, but it's clearly not encouraged.

The guides are reluctant even to let anglers handle the fish they catch. They weigh and unhook them in the net, handle them with gloves, revive and release them lovingly. When you want a photograph, you better do it quickly and respectfully. These trout are treasures.

★ ★ ★

In late July, darkness falls on Labrador around ten PM. The three hours after dinner are prime. If the wind lies down, the spinners will fall, and if the spinners fall, the big trout will come to the top to eat them.

We motor up to Big Hairy Lake, the headwaters of the Minipi system, sharp-eyed guide Gene Hart at the motor, anglers Andy Gill and I with our 4-weights locked and loaded. The lake has gone flat. A damp, chilly mist begins to fall. Typical of Labrador in July. We pull on rain jackets.

Gene cuts back the motor and we peer into a cove. "We got some bugs," he announces. There are spinners on the water, big brown drakes, dark wings still upright, silhouettes against the glassy glare. It's not a blanket spinnerfall. It rarely is, with the big mayflies. This is better. It's enough to bring up the fish, but not so heavy that our imitations will be lost amid the multitudes.

We chug around behind the islands, we drift through The Narrows. We are looking for the swirl of a feeding trout. One swirl will jump our adrenaline.

Then Gene grunts. He is pointing. Andy, from the bow, says, "Oh, yeah." I don't see it. Gene throttles up the motor, sprints a quarter of a mile across the lake, then cuts it, and we glide silently into the cove.

There's another swirl. I see it. It's about 100 feet away. "Comin' this way," mutters Gene. He turns us broadside to the fish with a flick of his paddle. Andy and I stand up and strip line off our reels. We've done this before. He'll drop his fly to his side of the swirl, leaving me a clear shot at my side. We will bracket the fish with our flies. We hope it will eat one of them. Neither of us much cares which one.

The trout swirls again, about 40 feet, two o'clock. Andy's drake spinner lands about two feet to the left of the swirl. Mine falls about four feet to the right. I sense the fish is headed my way, though I couldn't say why. Something about the shape of the swirl, the angle of the tail. I am tense, ready.

But instead it turns, lifts its back out of water, and eats Andy's fly with an audible "slurp." Andy tightens. His rod bends. "Heavy fish," he mumbles. The trout slogs and bores down, but Andy gets it into Gene's net after just a few minutes. On 2-X tippets we play these fish aggressively and try to net them before they're exhausted. We'd rather lose a fish than injure or weaken it.

This one is a fat female. Gene weighs her in his net. Seven pounds even.

We chase two more swirls before darkness spreads over the lake. The first one comes up a few times before we're in range, then disappears. That happens. We get two good shots at the second fish before it, too, stops playing our game.

We motor back to the lodge in the darkness, huddled in our parkas against the damp chill. We are satisfied. It was an excellent evening of trout fishing.

Around midnight we take a break from the poker table to watch the Northern Lights flash and flicker overhead.

★ ★ ★

In 1973 a biologist from Cornell studied the Minipi fish and concluded that they are comprised of two unique populations of brook trout. One group spends their lives in the rivers that connect the lakes. They mature at two years and rarely live more than four.

The other group, the lake dwellers, don't mature until they're four or five years old, and they often live for nine years. These fish typically grow to seven or eight pounds. Nine-pounders, while remarkable, are caught every year. Some experts believe that a trout to eclipse Dr. Cook's 14-pound 8-ounce Nipogon record presently lives somewhere in the Minipi drainage.

Nine IGFA line- and tippet-class world-record brook trout have come from the Minipi system, including the 10-pounder taken by Sal Borelli on 4-pound tippet in 1987.

The Minipi brookies have evolved their long-lived heavy-weight genes over tens of thousands of generations in a perfect brook-trout environment—limitless cold clean water, abundant forage, few predators, no competitors. Best of all, humans have left them alone. They are not pellet-fed hybrids or hatchery-made DNA freaks. These are natural, utterly wild creatures, perfectly adapted to their harsh world.

I keep coming back to their size because, after a few days of fishing for them, it's tempting to begin taking them for granted, to yawn at the 5-pounders, to feel disappointed that the 6½-pounder didn't drag the scale down to 7.

That would be a terrible mistake. Every single giant Minipi brook trout should be cherished.

The biggest brookie I ever caught in half a century of fishing in New England measured 15½ inches. It had no doubt been born in a hatchery.

The very first brook trout I hooked in Labrador weighed 2¾ pounds by the guide's scale. It looked to be about 18 inches long. It was a gorgeous fish, and the biggest brookie of my life.

The guide snorted as he tipped the fish out of his net. "That one don't count," he said. "Book fish gotta be three pound. Under three pound, just a baby."

It turned out to be the smallest Minipi trout I've ever caught.

★ ★ ★

Our camp is equipped with a satellite phone that occasionally works and a woodstove that throws out plenty of heat, which we appreciate after the sun sets. No telephone, no Internet, no television. It takes a day or two for busy men with high-stress jobs to adjust. We play poker every night. We tie flies. We read. One day merges into the next. Gradually, we relax.

Every morning after breakfast, three boats, each containing a guide and two anglers, disperse. Some head for the short portages to Big or Little Hairy. Some head down to the rapids at Shearpin or Big Red. Some decide to cruise Minonopi itself, or Green Pond. At different times of the season one or the other place heats up. The week before we arrived, the brown drakes were swarming on Green. Now the hatch seems to have moved up to Big Hairy.

We rarely spot rising fish in the mornings. Usually a breeze riffles the water, and it's too early in the day for mayflies to hatch anyway. We throw deerhair mice and streamers in the moving water at the lake outlets and in the mouths of feeder streams. Sometimes we add six inches of wire to our 8-weight outfits, tie on a big foam gurgler or yellow bass popper, and catch a bunch of pike. The pike are vicious, the perfect antidote for a slow morning of trout fishing. Average big ones range up to 7 or 8 pounds, and there are plenty of double-digit northerns in these lakes. We have no qualms about keeping a mess of pike. Andy knows how to filet the bones out of them, and Elliot and Steven, our gourmet cooks, usurp Sylvia's kitchen to prepare them for our table.

In the afternoon, some drakes usually hatch in the sheltered coves, and if it's not too windy—often it is too windy—we hunt down sipping trout and drop dry flies in front of them.

In the backs of our minds, we are anticipating the evening, hoping the wind dies and the spinners fall. It usually happens. It gets intense, hunting and chasing swirling trout, as the sun drops behind the spruce forest in the west and the moon rises in the east.

On our last evening in Labrador we linger after dark, reluctant to quit for good, all three boats parked in the Big Hairy outlet where a couple of trout are cruising in big circles, sipping fallen spinners. The moonlight catches the widening rings of each tiny dimple, and we aim blindly for them. We cannot see our flies on the water. We cannot even see the other boats. All nine of us—six anglers and three guides—talk among ourselves in the dark, alerting each other to a trout's riseform within casting distance.

Then—I don't know how I know, because I can't see anything, but I do know, for certain—I say, "Got 'im." I lift my rod, and the trout is on.

It's a male, 5½ pounds on Peter's scale, which we read by flashlight.

Murmurs of "way to go" and "nice fish" and "good way to end it" drift from the other boats. Then comes the soft chatter of reels taking in line, and the outboards start up, and all three boats chug back to camp. Tomorrow morning the Twin Otter will glide up to the dock and take us back to civilization.

18

Alas, the Bighorn

Andy and I made our first Montana Trout odyssey in the summer of 1986. It took us from the South Fork of the Snake to the Henry's Fork to the Box Canyon to Hebgen Lake to the Madison to the Yellowstone to Slough Creek to the Paradise Valley spring creeks. It was glorious and eye-opening for a pair of eastern dudes but, after almost two weeks of baking under a relentless Montana sun, fishing dawn-to-dark, driving by night, eating in the car, and sleeping in motels, we were kind of worn down. I wouldn't say we were sick of fishing. But the edge had definitely rubbed off.

We had saved the Bighorn for the end of our trip. If the stories were just half true, we would be rejuvenated.

★ ★ ★

Bill Rohrbacher, a big burly guy with a giant mug of coffee in his hand and shy grin peeking out of his tangled beard, took one look at us and said, "You boys're looking kinda used up. I got just the thing for you."

We rigged our rods and wadered up, and we launched Bill's driftboat for our first look at the Bighorn. It was one of those soft, gray, misty-moisty summer mornings, absolutely still, rare for Montana, the kind of morning that just feels fishy no matter what part of the world you're in. The water was scummy with bugs, and we saw dimples and noses and swirls all along the banks as Bill steered us downriver.

I pointed. "What about them?"

He smiled. "We got plenty of fish."

After ten or fifteen minutes, he rowed across the river, nosed the boat against a steep bank, and threw the anchor up into the bushes. "Behold," he said, gesturing upstream from where we sat.

It took me a minute to realize what I was seeing. At first it looked like a ten-foot swath of riffled water flowing against the bank and extending upriver into the mist.

Then I realized that the riffle effect was caused by feeding trout, hundreds of trout churning the water, poking up their noses, humping their dorsal fins, wagging their tails, turning and swirling and boiling. Big trout, judging by the size of their noses. Bill called them "toads." The snout of a big brown trout does look something like a toad when he pokes it up to eat a bug.

For the rest of the day, Andy and I took turns casting to those toads. It was just what we needed. While one of us fished to that pod of trout, the other one sat on the bank with Bill, smoking, sipping coffee, munching apples, telling stories, kibitzing, getting to know each other. Rarely did either of us need more than ten minutes to hook a trout. The trick, Bill said, was not to flock shoot. Pick a nose, learn his rhythm, then lay the tippet between his eyes.

I found that flock shooting actually worked pretty well, but I didn't tell Bill that.

The trout ran from about fifteen to nineteen fat healthy inches long. When they felt the hook, they exploded in the shallow water and surged for the heavy currents in the middle of the river. They were powerful, unstoppable fish on four-weight rods, and by the time we released them, the others were up and feeding again.

After a while, we got so we could pick out the 19-inch toads by the size of their snouts, and those were the ones we tried to catch.

It was dry-fly nirvana, and yet all the other boats we saw on the river that day were drifting down the middle dragging pink strike indicators.

"Oh, no doubt, it's a great nymph river," Bill told us. "You can catch a boatful on scud and sowbug imitations if that's what you want, and most of the guides, well, they can put their clients into plenty of fish that way without hardly breaking a sweat. Rig 'em up, throw it over the side, and go floating down the river. But lookit that." He waved at the lineup of big trout noses. "Who'd want to drag lead when you got that?"

The next day we fished with Dave Schuller, Bill's partner. Dave was small and quick and athletic and bubbling with energy and enthusiasm, the Southern California yin to Bill's laid-back Northern California yang. He must have beached his boat at twenty places. Move it, let's go, climb out, cast quick, come on, catch a few, that's it, back in the boat, next spot. There were rising fish everywhere Dave stopped, pods of big brown trout eating pale morning duns. He wanted to catch them all. Just about the time the PMD hatch petered out, black caddis began swarming, and the water became crusty with them. The trout switched over, and so did we. We fished into darkness. Dave didn't want to quit. There were still fish to catch.

★ ★ ★

When I got home and had time to sort it out, I realized that by all the standards I could think of, the Bighorn had to be the best dry-fly river—maybe the best trout river—in the world. Where else could you absolutely depend on finding fish up to and over twenty inches—hundreds of trout, if you knew where to look—sipping mayflies and caddis off the surface all day, every day? Certainly none of the other legendary western rivers I'd fished even came close.

I looked it up. There were 8500 trout per mile in the Bighorn's upper thirteen miles that summer, of which half were over thirteen inches, making it probably the most densely populated trout river in the history of trout rivers. With the even tailwater flows, the fertile weedy water, and the abundant forage, the fish grew at the astonishing rate of six inches a year.

I wrote an article called "Bighorn of Plenty" for *Field & Stream*. Bill and Dave got prominent mention and presumably more business, so they insisted that thereafter we fish with them as partners, not clients.

Andy and I spent ten days to two weeks in Montana every summer after that first one. We always arranged our Fish-Til-You-Puke-Trout-Bombing-Mission so that the best—a few days on the Bighorn with Bill and Dave—came last. We learned the river's hotspots—the Owl Tree, Spring Creek, Glory Hole, the

Bluffs, Pipeline. We knew the best runs for throwing early-morning streamers, the best riffles for mid-morning nymphing, the best scumlines for mid-day PMDs, the best banks for afternoon sippers, and the best flats for evening caddis.

Andy usually paired up with Dave. They liked to fish hard and compete with each other. I generally fished with Bill. Sometimes we just sat under a cottonwood sipping coffee and watching the water and telling stories. He told me that everybody called him Bubba, and I should, too, and there was no sense in making a joke out of it, because he'd heard them all and was immune to being offended.

He called me Grandfather, because I was almost ten years older than him, and I wasn't offended.

Bubba taught me how to row a driftboat, how to spot the tiny blippy riseforms of bank-sipping browns, how to cast long trout tippets straight into the wind, how to land and unhook big trout without a net. The PMDs began popping every morning at eleven, and after the hatch petered out we could always find fish eating leftovers along the weed patties and in the scumlines and backwaters, and pretty soon the black caddis would start popping and continue into the darkness. More often than not we ended up fishing by moonlight and then racing to get to Polly's for our ribeye steaks before she closed.

After a while, I think Andy and I could have done a decent job of guiding dry-fly anglers on the Bighorn.

One July evening as the four of us were speeding back to Fort Smith in Bubba's ancient Power Wagon, late for dinner as usual, I said, "Let's make a pact. We four will fish the Bighorn together every summer till one of us dies."

"That's a long time, Grandfather," said Bubba.

"I hope it is," I said.

"Things change," Dave said. "Nobody understands the life cycle of tailwaters. This river's just a baby. Who knows how long it'll last?"

"Don't talk that way," I said.

"*Carpe diem*," said Andy.

"We got great carp fishing in the reservoir," said Bubba.

For several years, the Bighorn did not change. Oh, the boat traffic became ridiculous as the word got around (I suppose my article didn't help). But the hatches came like clockwork, and big brown trout ate bugs off the surface all day, every day. You could plan your trip a year ahead and know exactly what to expect.

And that's what Andy and I and thousands of other trout fishermen did, and none of us was ever disappointed. By the early nineties, a hundred boats were launched on the Bighorn every summer's day. A village of fly shops had sprung up in Fort Smith. Dozens of trout guides worked the river. Most of them rigged their clients with nymphs and strike indicators and split shot and left the dry-fly fishing to Bubba and Dave. Everybody caught tons of trout.

If you launched early enough, you could get there first and stake out a prime piece of water, and you'd find the fishing almost as good as it had been back in '86. Those who counted them reported that the trout density was declining—5000 fish per mile in 1991 was a big falloff in just five years—but it was still an awful lot of trout.

Dave was right. Things did change. There were high-water years and low-water years and some years when you got both.

The fluctuating water levels affected the insects and the fish. One year the PMDs, which used to begin hatching in late July, started in mid-June and petered out after a few weeks. One September, just a dribble of tricos hatched right at sunup. The hatch merged with the spinnerfall and lasted barely an hour, and for the rest of the day, we searched the Bighorn for rising trout and didn't spot a single bank sipper.

The Bighorn was stone dead. It was a spooky sight.

★ ★ ★

Andy and I returned to Fort Smith for the last time in the summer of '97, our twelfth year at the Bighorn. Dave, discouraged by the river's decline, had left by then. We stayed in Bubba's house. He had clients, but his friend and fellow guide Don Cooper took us down the river. The water was high. There were no PMDs to speak of, even though it was late July, formerly prime time. The tricos had started already, more than a month early. Coop said that was a bad sign. But we had fun and caught a few trout, and we became friends, the way you do when you spend time on a river together and the fishing isn't very good.

★ ★ ★

That fall Bubba called to tell me that one of his clients had offered him a real job, and he was going to take it, sell his boat, and move to Atlanta. Health insurance, pension, stock options, sick days, salary? Hey, you can't be a fishing guide all your life.

It was unclear who he was trying to convince.

★ ★ ★

The drought has been severe in the west the past several years. All the rivers are suffering. Several of my friends go to Fort Smith every year, and they tell me the Bighorn's still a fabulous trout river. They rig up with strike indicators and split shot and dredge the channels, and they catch 'em on scuds and sowbugs. The trout are running bigger than ever. Rainbows, mostly. There aren't that many browns anymore. Twenty-two, twenty-four-inchers are not uncommon.

What about the dry-fly fishing?

Oh, you hardly ever see rising fish anymore, my sources tell me. The tricos and PMDs and black caddis come off unpredictably and sparsely, if at all, and the trout pretty much ignore them.

I don't like to dwell on the past. Dave was right, of course. Nothing stays the same. I know that. But some things just change too much, and too fast.

★ ★ ★

Dave and Coop are dead now. They were both young men, and they went suddenly and unexpectedly.

Bubba's working in the Bahamas. He goes bonefishing on his days off.

He called just last week. He'd had some awesome permit fishing in the Turks and Caicos, he said, and he'd found some secret bonefish flats near Grand Bahama.

"But I miss the trout, Grandfather," he said.

"I really don't want to go back to the Bighorn," I said.

"It's all scuds and sowbugs," said Bubba. "Big rainbows, right on the bottom. I talked to Mike the other day. He told me they've got to pinch on so much lead that they're blowing up party balloons and using 'em for strike indicators."

"Balloons on the Bighorn," I said. "Jesus."

"Yeah," said Bubba, "but Mike said they were getting better flows last summer. He told me he actually found a few fish eating black caddis one night. Wouldn't that be something?"

"If the dry-fly fishing comes back?" I said. "PMDs and tricos and black caddis? You kidding?"

"It might," he said. "Like Dave used to say. Things change."

"If it does," I said, "Andy and I will meet you in Fort Smith. *Carpe diem*, man."

"I got no interest in carp, Grandfather."

19

The Norfork Tailwater

You'll find Norfork, Arkansas, population 494, nestled deep in the Ozarks at the confluence of the White and North Fork rivers halfway between Flippin and Calico Rock, about twenty miles from the Missouri border. As you cross the town line, you are greeted by a billboard-sized sign that reads: Welcome to Norfork, Arkansas, Home of the World Record Brown Trout, 38 Pounds 9 Ounces.

That behemoth measured 41 inches long and had a girth of 27¾ inches. The great fish was caught from the Norfork Tailwater in August 1988 on a small treble hook impaled with kernels of canned corn and drifted on the bottom. It remains the town of Norfork's main claim to fame.

When the lucky fisherman reeled it in and saw what he had, he called local trout guru John Gulley for help. Gulley put a tape to that record brown and couldn't help chuckling.

A few days earlier he'd taken Arthur Hempsted out for some night fishing. Hempsted was a specialist at catching big trout on light fly tackle at night. The Norfork Tailwater was his favorite destination, and John Gulley was his favorite guide.

"Arthur was using a size 12 wet fly and 4X tippet and a 5-weight rod," remembers Gulley. "When he hooked that fish, he just gentled him over to a sand bar so I could corral him. I don't think the fish ever realized he'd been hooked. Arthur was awfully good at catching big fish. In the light of my flashlight, this one looked huge. I told Arthur it was way over 30 pounds. He said, 'I always thought if I caught one over 25 pounds I'd kill it and have it mounted.' I said, 'What do you want me to do?' and he said, 'Let him go.' So I measured him and released him. Next thing I knew, there he was again. Same fish. Identical measurements. A world record brown, as it turned out. Arthur never seemed to regret putting him back, though."

The record stood until 1992, when a 40-pound 4-ounce brown was taken from the nearby Little Red River. The Norfork fish remains the second-largest ever caught anywhere.

★ ★ ★

That record trout was not a fluke (pun noted, but incidental). Six days after the record brown was caught, a local fisherman took one from the Norfork that weighed 34 pounds 4 ounces. The Norfork Tailwater is probably the best place in North America to catch a truly humungous brown or rainbow trout on a fly. The brookies and cutthroats grow big, too.

I do not exaggerate. The Norfork joins the mighty White River at the town of Norfork, infusing it with cold water and luring big White River trout into its channels. In summer and fall, White River browns and brookies and resident Norfork fish follow their spawning urges up the river toward the hatchery on

Dry Run Creek, a Norfork tributary, where they were born. In winter and spring, rainbows and cutts do the same thing. When I fished the Norfork Tailwater in late June, some of the browns we caught were already showing their spawning colors.

Young trout grow at the astonishing rate of one inch per month in the Norfork. There are many reasons for this. It's a tailwater, with cool well-oxygenated water from the bottom of the reservoir and constant ideal water temperatures year round. The river cuts through limestone hills and valleys, making it exceptionally fertile. Sowbugs and scuds, trout staples, blanket every rock and weed stem and leaf in the river. There are loads of crawfish, creek chubs and sculpins. Mayflies, caddisflies, midges and craneflies hatch in abundance. Plus, every winter Norfork Lake, the reservoir that feeds the Norfork Tailwater, undergoes a mysterious phenomenon that locals call "the shad kill." Tons of threadfin shad, the predominant baitfish in the lake, get sucked into the hydroelectric turbines where they're diced and sliced and spewed into the North Fork. Trout chow. Local fish fatten up.

The Norfork is the only river I know where you can legitimately anticipate a 10-pound trout on any cast. Your best chances are on low water at night, when the Army Corps of Engineers, which controls the dam and its releases, generally holds back water. Big trout of all four species prowl the shallows, especially on cloudy, moonless nights. If you're in the right place, swinging a woolly bugger or a muddler through the currents at the right time . . .

Usually it doesn't happen, of course. I fished the Norfork Tailwater two June nights in a row, midnight to sunup. I caught about a dozen fish each night, none over 20 inches. Nice fish, but not the certifiable Big One I was hoping for, although I did hook a couple that sounded truly big.

In the dark, you learn to judge the size of a fish by the timbre and volume of the slosh it makes when you first hook it. On our second night my partner Pat, standing 30 yards downstream from me, landed browns of 25 and 29 inches in rapid succession. The second fish, he estimated, weighed about 12 pounds. I heard the sloshes his trout made. I believe I hooked a couple that big.

★ ★ ★

The water levels in the Norfork vary dramatically. The flows are unpredictable and at the whim of the Corps, but generally speaking, when Norfork Lake is high (as it usually is in the spring and early summer), the times of high water are more frequent and longer-lasting.

When both gates are closed, the river resembles a placid spring creek. It flows low and crystal clear, and you can navigate all of it in waders. There are riffles, runs, and pools, and everywhere sight-fishing opportunities for nymphing trout. Mayflies, midges, and caddisflies hatch on low water, offering the best chance for hatch-matching dry-fly fishing.

Even when the Corps is running a lot of water, they generally shut it down at night. Swinging streamers and wet flies through low-water currents at night is fun and deadly. At daybreak the trout become active on midges, and it's worth switching to a sight-fishing setup.

They blow a siren to announce the opening of a gate and the release of water from the dam. Don't hesitate. Get the hell out of there promptly. In a matter of minutes the gentle little Norfork Tailwater is transformed into a big brawling river. On high water it looks daunting and unfishable, but, in fact, the fishing can be terrific then.

John Gulley has developed a lethal method for catching the big fish that rub their bellies on the riverbottom in high water. You brace yourself in the bow of his specially-designed motorized Norfork boat. You're rigged with a San Juan Worm or a Glo Bug, a split-shot the size of a mothball six inches up the leader, a bulky strike indicator ten feet up from the fly, and a 6- or 7-weight rod. Heave it (you don't really *cast* this rig) up into the current seams and through the runs and along the edges of the sunken grass beds, while John maneuvers the boat to maximize your drift. Mend constantly and, when the indicator darts under, as it will frequently, set the hook with a sharp sideways jerk.

When only one gate is open and the water isn't quite so high, muddlers and woolly buggers on sinking lines, and even floating cranefly imitations, will take some of those big fish. Cast toward the banks, along current seams, and over grass beds.

★ ★ ★

It's tantalizing to know that on any given cast you might catch a 12-incher or a 12-pounder. The big ones are there all year, but you don't have to be a big-trout fanatic to enjoy excellent year-round fishing on the Norfork. The river is stocked frequently, and there are always loads of fish in the 13- to 19-inch range.

Winter: Snow and freezing temperatures are unusual in the Ozarks. Most days you can fish without discomfort, and in the winter the river runs low for long periods of time. Midges hatch every day, offering excellent sight fishing with larva and pupa imitations and sometimes dry flies. Norfork trout feed on sowbugs and scuds year round. On the right kind of day, you'll find superior dry-fly fishing to a blue-winged olive hatch.

Spring: In March caddisflies begin to show up—first blacks and olives, and toward April, green and tan bugs—along with comfortable fishing temperatures. The BWOs and midges continue to hatch, and sowbugs and scuds remain important. In May and June come excellent mayfly hatches—sulfurs (sizes 16 and 18) and pale morning duns (size 20).

Summer: The high July and August temperatures in the Ozarks, coupled with oppressive humidity, often make daytime fishing on the Norfork uncomfortable. Then it's time to go night fishing—always with a local angler or guide who's familiar with the river and its trout as well as the whims of the Army Corps. Big tailwater trout feed day and night, but in the summer they are particularly active after dark on low water. Local night-fishing specialists look for overcast. They stay home on bright moonlit summer nights.

Autumn: Tourists come to the Ozarks in the fall just to view the spectacular foliage. Fishermen come to the Norfork to catch aggressive, spawn-minded brown trout. Sight fishing with nymphs on low water remains productive, but in the fall fast-stripped streamers work well under all conditions. The gorgeous foliage and the comfortable daytime temperatures are a bonus.

★ ★ ★

I was embarrassed to tell my guides and the other local folks I met in Norfork, Arkansas that I knew very little about the Norfork Tailwater. But they didn't seem surprised. The big White, half a mile wide and a hundred miles long, and the nearby Little Red, where the current world-record brown trout was taken, get most of the publicity.

The Norfork Tailwater is only 4½ miles long, and even under a full head of water, it's barely fifty yards across. But it is perhaps the most interesting trout river I have ever fished. Its face changes constantly—high to low water, high to low light, day to night, season to season. It is loaded with trout, and especially with large trout. The current state record brook trout, a 5-pounder, was taken from the Norfork in 2002. No one would be surprised if the next world-record brown trout lives there.

And there are all those 10-plus pounders sloshing around out there. I can still hear them.

20

Trout in the Land of the Big Feet

O n the morning of our fourth day in Patagonia, we tugged on our waders and packed our gear for a forced march to the other end of the big *lago*, where we hoped to find some trout and a little shelter from the wind.

We knew the trout would be there, but the prospect of escaping the wind did not seem promising. Whitecaps were rolling across *Lago Trolope*. Now and then a gust of that legendary Patagonian gale would lift clouds of spindrift off the surface. This was the wind that had caused Antoine de Saint-Exupery's single-engine plane to fly backward. The British travel writer Bruce Chatwin described it as "stripping men to the raw." He meant laying bare their souls, but it was also possible to imagine this wind peeling off a man's skin.

Wind, of course, is the big enemy of fly fishermen every-where, but after a few days in Patagonia, we'd begun to conjure with it. It was a constant, unrelenting variable, and you just dealt with it. You looked for a little lee. You put the wind at your back. You kept your backcast low and your hat in your pocket, and you cupped your flybox against your chest when you opened it the way you'd protect a match to light a cigarette.

There was no evidence that the wind bothered the trout.

We were hoping for some dry-fly action. There were flats at the far end of the lake. At mid-day in the late summer, according to Martin, mayflies sometimes hatched off those flats and, when they did, if they weren't blown away first, big browns and rainbows cruised around and gobbled them off the surface.

We clambered up and down hills and over lava rock, we slogged through mud, and we detoured around clumps of scrubby *jarilla* bushes. It was a *muy grand lago*. A long hike in waders.

A few miles to our west, so close in that vast empty landscape that you felt you could reach over and touch them, the Andes that demarcate the Argentine-Chilean border jutted up suddenly from the plains like the jagged spine of some half-buried prehistoric skeleton. A rumbling snow-streaked volcano loomed over the head of the lake. Off to the east, the windswept desert rolled away to a horizon made blurry by clouds of wind-blown dust.

In Patagonia, you don't worry about fishing pressure. You worry about disappearing. Whether you're standing in a river or hiking around a lake, the landscape has a way of reminding you how far from home you are, how puny, how insignificant, how isolated. It makes you want to hug your friends and stick close to your guide. The writer Nicholas Shakespeare said, "Travelers from Darwin onward have noted how this bleakness seizes the imagination. Patagonia's nothingness forces the mind in on itself."

Everything in Patagonia seems outsized. When Magellan explored the region in 1520, he reported that the typical native person was "so tall that we reached only to his waist," and so he called the region Patagoni— "Land of the big feet."

High above us, three condors were circling on their ten-foot wingspans. I told Martin they probably had their eye on us.

"Condors are no worry, man, as long as you stay alive." He pointed down at the mud. "But watch out for Senor Puma."

I squatted down and examined the paw prints. They were the size of my big-arbor fly reel, bigger than life, like the condors and everything else in Patagonia.

★ ★ ★

Lago Trolope forms the headwaters of *Rio Trolope*, an intimate trout river by Argentine standards that in many places reminded me of my beloved Paradise Valley spring creeks. *R. Trolope* meanders through private ranchland for about fifteen miles, opening in two places into lagoons before joining *R. Agrio*, a pretty river that's sterile and fishless due to centuries of sulfurous eruptions from the still-active *Copahue* volcano. At the little bed-and-breakfast in the village of Caviahue, where we made our headquarters, the rumbling of the volcano was a constant that made our sleep uneasy the first night, but thereafter faded into the background.

The five of us—four Boston shrinks and one New Hampshire ne'r-do-well—had been lured to this northwestern corner of Argentine Patagonia by the opportunity to cast flies into a virtually virgin trout river. According to Martin Carranza, our guide and outfitter, the Trolope had only been "discovered" a few years earlier, when an off-course Andes skier reported spotting this delicious-looking stream to his friend Gustavo Southart. Gustavo, a trout-fishing enthusiast and all-round competent person (Martin calls him "Chris" after Christopher Reeve, whom Gustavo resembles both in appearance and in his Superman conditioning and all-round competence), got permission from the rancher, who owns all of the land surrounding the lake and the river, then fished its entire length.

The river, Gustavo found, held a healthy population of good-sized trout. Mostly rainbows, but plenty of browns, and the occasional brookie, too. Some of the browns were very large.

Gustavo shared his find with his friend Martin, who bargained with the rancher for exclusive guiding rights on the Trolope.

We were just the third party to fish there with Martin and Gustavo.

With people, virginity is an either-or proposition. But with trout rivers, it doesn't get much closer to virginal than that.

★ ★ ★

We left snowy Boston at two on a Friday afternoon in the first week of March— dead winter still in New England— and 24 hours later we were in Patagonia. It was a complicated itinerary, changing planes in Miami, a nine-hour overnight flight to Buenos Aires, a headlong taxi ride to catch another flight from a different airport on the other side of the city, two more hours in the air, then a half-hour's drive to Junin de los Andes, our first destination in Patagonia.

Flowers were blooming. Birds were singing. It was summertime in the southern hemisphere.

Junin de los Andes is known and famed for its nearby trout rivers—*Rio Chimehuin, R. Malleo, R. Alumine, R. Collon Cura.* Miles and miles of freestone trout water so pure you can drink it. The walls of the little inn where we stayed were plastered with photographs of both famous and anonymous anglers hoisting the 20- and 30-pound trout that they'd taken from these waters. I recognized Joe Brooks and Al McClane.

Jet-lagged and sleep-deprived, we fished the *Malleo,* the smallest and most intimate of the area rivers, that first afternoon. I wandered upstream by myself and stumbled upon a flat pool where some fish were rising, and once I figured out that trout are everywhere trout and don't feel obligated to eat the first thing you throw at them no matter how far you might have traveled to get there, I caught a few. They were fat, healthy rainbows ranging from a foot to about 17 inches long.

We fished til dark, drove back to the inn, and walked to a nearby restaurant, where I made several discoveries:

1. If you can't speak Spanish, no matter how clever you are with your hands, you cannot communicate with Argentinians outside of Buenos Aires. I depended on Martin and Gustavo to translate for me and quickly learned how to order what for me are the restaurant essentials— *grand cafe solo* (large coffee without milk) and *agua sin gas* (non-carbonated water). All the rest remained a mystery.

2. In Buenos Aires restaurants, the steaks are thick, juicy and tender. In the Patagonian villages, the beef comes overcooked, unchewable, and tasteless. I'd looked forward to Argentinian beef. It was my biggest—my only—disappointment.

3. The local wines, on the other hand, lived up to their billing.

4. When in doubt, order *Parrilladas,* an Argentinian mixed grill consisting of hunks of goat meat, lamb, *pollo*, various sausages, and, yes beef. A big grill mounded with charcoal-broiled meats is placed in the middle of your table, enough for seven hungry men. Everybody helps himself. The goat was pretty good.

5. Patagonian breakfasts consist of juice and coffee and a variety of breads and buns and scones with marmalade and jam. Not an egg or a rasher of bacon in sight.

6. In Patagonia, no merchant accepts American money. Most towns have outdoor ATM machines that dispense pesos from U.S. bank cards. The exchange rate was about three pesos to the dollar. Dinner at a restaurant—salad, entree, coffee, dessert—cost about 20 pesos.

7. The local people are uniformly friendly and open, and if you can say *hola, buenas dias, por favor,* and *gracias*, no matter how amusing your accent, they will smile and try to help you.

8. You can arrange with your cell-phone company for service from Argentina, but you'll pay several dollars for every minute, even when your call doesn't go through. Public phone service, on the other hand, is a thriving business in the Patagonian villages. Go to one of the little storefronts, sign up for a booth, dial 001 and the number, and you can talk to New Hampshire for ten minutes for about three pesos.

★ ★ ★

On our second morning in Patagonia we drove northwest from Junin de los Andes to Caviahue, our headquarters for fishing *Rio*

Trolope. Five hours across the Patagonian desert, and except for a lone gaucho herding a flock of sheep alongside the road and three scattered, sleepy villages, the landscape was empty—just flat basalt plains and distant mountains punctuated with mesas and buttes and arroyos and a few cottonwood-lined streams. Our first long view of Patagonia. Awesome, beautiful, desolate, unforgiving. Seeing it forced me to imagine how the earliest settlers might have felt when they rolled onto the endless plains of the American West with the purple Rockies rising on the faraway horizon.

We settled into our little Caviahue bed-and-breakfast in the shadow of the rumbling volcano, then drove to the ranch for our first look at *Rio Trolope*. We hiked upstream and waded our way back down. We threw streamers on 6-weight rods and sink-tip lines and hit fish in all the likely places—current seams, eddies, pools, brush-lined cut banks. They ran from about 14 to 20 inches, mostly rainbows. I rolled a brown in a bend pool that stopped my breath. He showed me a broad buttery flank that reminded me of the photos on the wall at the inn.

Andy hooked one that jumped several time before it came unbuttoned. Five or 6 pounds, we guessed.

The upper section was classic pool-riffle-run water. It twisted through the low hills and showed a different face at every turn. As the sun sank and we worked our way back to where the truck was parked, the river flattened out and became distinctly spring-creeky—slow, flat, and deep.

Here and there a fish rose to some unfamiliar sparsely hatching mayfly. "Gray All-Day Duns," Martin called them with a smile. I couldn't identify them, either, but an Adams or a blue-wing olive imitation did the job. He said this mystery mayfly hatched intermittently throughout the late summer (February and March).

The moment the sun sank behind the Andes, the air temperature plummeted. But the wind persisted. This was Patagonia in late summer. It didn't stop the fish from feeding, and it didn't stop us from trying to catch them, until it was too dark to change flies.

We explored other sections of the fifteen miles of R. *Trolope* during the three days we were there. We found the greatest concentrations of trout in those long slow pools where the reed-lined banks were high and the water ran deep. We had most of our success twitching cone-head woolly buggers and bunny flies and Gartside soft hackles along the bottom.

Toward the end of each afternoon, we found some fish rising to Gray All-Day Duns and, at dusk, just for the fun of it, I liked to throw a big Serendipity against the reeds and chug it across the surface like a bass bug. Those rainbows would come slashing at it. Dead-drifting an elk-hair caddis with a prince nymph dropper worked well top and bottom.

★ ★ ★

"Bigger fish in the *lago*," Martin had promised. It kept me going during that long hike.

There wasn't much lee at the far end when we finally got there, nor did we spot any fish rising in the chop. So we put our back to the wind and muscled woolly buggers over the dropoffs and caught many trout. They did seem to run bigger in the lake—16 or 17 inches on average, with some creeping into the plus-twenty-inch range.

Martin disappeared around a point of land. When he came back he held up his hand and made biting motions. Rising fish. He waved us to follow him.

The dark-bottomed flat was as big as two or three soccer fields. Here the wind was blowing the tops off the rolling waves, and it took a minute to distinguish the whitecaps from the boiling, slashing trout. I bent close to the water and saw the brownish mayflies—size 16, I estimated. I guessed *Callibaetis*. Martin identified them as Mahogany Duns. His favorite all-purpose dry fly, a parachute pheasant tail, imitated them. So did my parachute Adams.

It took a while to figure it out. First, I had to wade in up to my knees to feel steady on my feet with that great wind trying to knock me on my face. Then I had to abandon normal flycasting and go with the roll cast. With the wind at my back, it took just a flick of the wrist to roll-cast 60 or 70 feet. I gave up the idea of targeting any particular one of those big cruising trout. Throw it out there, let it bob on the rollers, and pretty soon a trout would come along and eat it. More often than not, the fish struck when the white-winged dry fly was drifting down the far side of a wave and I couldn't see the take.

For a couple of hours, it was glorious. Andy landed and measured a 24-incher. I broke off two that looked to be about that size, and I spotted a few others rolling and swirling for mayflies that were surely bigger.

Later, as we made the long trek around the lake back to the truck, I said to Martin, "I suppose you local guys are so used to the wind that you don't even notice it."

He smiled and waved his hand at the white-capped water. "That, *senor*, is a very big wind. I have not seen wind like that in a long time. But," he added with a shrug, "this is Patagonia."

21

Volkswagen Cove

In the last month of my father's life, when he knew his days were numbered, fishing memories comforted and sustained him. He'd had a good life, he said. No regrets. He'd been pretty lucky.

I knew I'd been lucky, too. Dad and I never had any of those silent agendas and unspoken tensions between us that so many men seem to have with their fathers. We'd been best friends from the beginning.

One afternoon when I went into his bedroom, I found him lying there with his eyes closed and a smile on his face.

I pulled up a chair. "You sleeping?" I said.

He blinked his eyes open. "Nope. I was just thinking about that week on Upper Dobsis. How long ago was that?"

"Over fifty years, I guess."

He nodded. "Remember Volkswagen Cove?"

★ ★ ★

We fished together as a family, my mother and father and little sister and I, once a year, on a wilderness lake in northeastern

Maine, a different one each summer, for the one week in early July that Dad took for his vacation from the wars he fought in the city the other fifty-one weeks.

My father, of course, loved fishing. It was never clear to me how my mother and sister felt about it, although the fact that they didn't fish at all aside from that single week in July was a clue.

Actually, typical of a not-quite-teenaged boy, I didn't care about anybody else. I was obsessed with fishing. For me, this was the best week of the year.

★ ★ ★

It was an all-day car ride from our home in eastern Massachusetts to that part of Maine. The turnpike ended in Augusta in those days, and after that we bumped over winding two-lane country roads through the dusty summer countryside for several hours.

That particular summer, our lake was near the end of an unpaved logging road owned by the paper company. Dad's friend George Smith, an old-time Maine guide whom I called Uncle George, had permission to use it. Uncle George had built the log cabin on the other side of the lake by sledding everything except the logs across the ice in the winter. He kept a big Grand Lake canoe hidden in the bushes where the road passed closest to the lake.

So late in the afternoon, after that long day of family togetherness in the car, the four of us loaded a week's worth of food and fishing gear and clothing and bedding and games and books into the canoe, and we paddled across the lake to the one-room cabin on the other shore.

It came equipped with two sets of bunk beds, a table with four chairs, knives and forks, plates and glasses, an icebox, three kerosene lanterns, a wood stove, and a soapstone sink with a manual water pump. Four rickety wooden rocking chairs sat on the porch for watching the loons. There was an icehouse and a two-hole outhouse out back.

Twenty years earlier this lake, like all the other cold-water lakes in northeastern Maine, teemed with landlocked salmon. My father had fished there then with Uncle George. They trolled Grey Ghosts and Supervisors and Warden's Worrys behind their canoe, and I think Dad's memories of the fabulous salmon fishing on these lakes, which no one but George Smith and his sports fished, were what kept luring him up there.

But by the time we started going to Maine as a family, white perch and smallmouth bass had invaded the entire watershed. The perch and the bass were more aggressive and more adaptable than the salmon. They foraged on the smelt that were the salmon's main food source, and they probably foraged on baby salmon, too, and now you could troll all day without hooking a single salmon.

My father was philosophical about it. Everything changes, he said. Anyway, we came here mainly to have fun as a family, not to fish for landlocked salmon.

The decline of the salmon fishing didn't bother me. I didn't have my father's memories of it. I thought white perch and smallmouth bass were swell.

★ ★ ★

We spent the entire first day circling the shoreline in the canoe. "Getting the lay of the land," Dad said, meaning the water. Commenting on the area's pristine wildness, he observed that it was a place "where the hand of man has never set foot." My father, no Yogi Berra, mixed his metaphors with a purpose.

My mother and sister trolled streamers. I sat in the bow, casting toward the rocky shore. Dad paddled. We didn't expect to catch much, and we didn't. A few sausage-sized smallmouths latched onto the streamer I was casting. Twice that day the trolled streamers intercepted a school of white perch, and my mother and sister brought in two or three apiece in rapid succession. Dad circled back so I could cast to them, and I caught few, too, before the schools went down.

We kept twelve of them for dinner. White perch freshly caught from a clean cold lake and filleted and fried in butter over a campfire, said Dad, were the best-eating fish in the world, and after we completed our circuit of the lake that afternoon, he proved it.

After supper, he looked at me and said, "Who wants to go fishing?"

My mother and sister rolled their eyes. Eight hours in a canoe was enough for one day.

"Me," I said.

The summer sun hung low in the sky, and the water's surface lay as flat as wet glass. Dad headed diagonally across the lake. He paddled hard, in a hurry, and the canvas-covered canoe hissed through the water. He said he'd noticed something earlier in the day that deserved a closer look.

We drifted into a big cove. It covered four or five acres, as I recall, and it was studded with giant boulders. Back then, I'd never seen a Volkswagen. But, in later years, Dad and I recalled that those round boulders looked like half-submerged Beetles, and we started remembering the place as Volkswagen Cove.

He tossed me a deerhair bass bug. "Tie that on and cast it out there," he said, and when I fumbled with the knot, he said, "Come *on*. Let's *go*," and I knew something had excited him.

I lobbed the bug against one of those big boulders, let it sit, gave it enough of a twitch to make it burble, let it sit . . . and the water under it imploded. The bass bent my rod double and leapt several times and, when I finally managed to stick my thumb in its mouth and lift it from the water, I saw that it was easily the biggest smallmouth bass I'd ever caught. Accounting for the passage of half a century, and in the interest of caution, I'll remember it as a 4-pounder, though I bet it was closer to 5.

I held it up and showed it to Dad.

He nodded. "Put it back and get that bug out there. It's getting dark."

One or two smallmouths lived beside every boulder. They were all about the size of that first one, and they walloped those deerhair bugs.

When darkness had fallen over the lake and Dad said we better head back to the cabin, we'd only fished a small part of the cove.

In the mornings and afternoons of that week, the four of us had ourselves a relaxing family vacation. Sometimes we trolled streamers from the canoe. Sometimes we drifted and dangled worms over the side. Sometimes we just turned our faces up to the sun and trailed our fingers in the water. We swam, we napped, we picnicked, we poked around in the woods. We read, we played cards, we told stories.

But every evening after supper, Dad and I paddled as fast as we could across the lake to Volkswagen Cove, and every evening monster smallmouths—no small ones—were waiting, eager to pounce on our deerhair bass bugs.

★ ★ ★

Dad had his eyes closed, remembering. "Best bass fishing of my life," he said. "And it's been a long life, full of fish."

"Best bass fishing of my life, too," I said. I hesitated. "There's something I never told you."

He smiled. "I'm not surprised."

"After three or four evenings on Volkswagen Cove," I said, "I was kinda wishing we could try someplace different. I mean, it was great. But it was—"

"A sure thing," said Dad.

"Exactly. After a while, knowing exactly what it was going to be, even as great as it was, it got a little, well, boring."

"How come you didn't say something?"

"I thought you'd be disappointed," I said. "You seemed to be having so much fun."

"That's pretty funny," he said. "I felt the same way. Kept going back because of you. A sure thing, no matter how good it is, wears thin after a while." Dad turned his head on his pillow and smiled. "I'm glad we finally cleared the air between us."

PART V

Fly-fishing Conundrums

"A man can be a fish hog with a fly rod as easily as he can with a cane pole. Easier perhaps."
—H. G. Tapply, *The Sportsman's Notebook*

"As the old fisherman remarked after explaining the various ways to attach a frog to a hook, it's all the same to the frog."
—Paul Schullery, *Mountain Time*

"People who fish for food, and sport be damned, are called pot-fishermen. The more expert ones are called crack pot-fishermen. All other fishermen are called crackpot fishermen. This is confusing."
—Ed Zern, *How To Tell Fish From Fishermen*

22

Thinkin' Mean

A late-May evening at the Powerline Pool on the Willow-emoc. I was blowing on my fly after releasing another nice 16-inch brown when a nearby angler reeled up and waded over towards me. He was a lanky middle-aged guy, salt-and-pepper stubble, shapeless felt hat. I'd noticed his casting stroke. Smooth. I'd also noticed that he wasn't catching any fish.

"Hey, fella," he said. "You got the secret fly, I can see that. Mind telling me what you're using?"

My first thought was: "Figure it out for yourself, *fella*. It's taken me years of aggravation to understand this hatch and find the right flies for it. Why should I make it easy for you?"

★ ★ ★

Pale Evening Duns. Little sulphurs. *Ephemerella dorothea.* They are lovely mayflies, delicate, pale yellow, size 18 or 20. In certain pools on the Willowemoc, in the heart of the Catskills on a soft evening in late May or early June, the little sulphurs begin to pop about two hours before sunset.

It's my favorite hatch. It's predictable, it's lavish, and it brings every trout in the pool to the surface.

For several seasons the Catskill sulphur hatch frustrated me. All around me trout would be gobbling mayflies. I'd isolate a little yellow natural, watch it drift down, see a brownish-gold shadow lift under it, watch a nose tilt up, a white mouth open, the bug disappear. I'd float an identical (to my eye) imitation down the same current, over the same fish, see his shadow materialize and drift under it . . . and then he'd sink back out of sight.

Frustrating, yeah. But fascinating, mesmerizing, and exciting, too. The first few times I found myself surrounded by tiny yellow sailboats and gorging trout I behaved badly. Once I realized that I wasn't going to catch every rising fish I covered—wasn't, maybe, going to catch any of them—I cursed the fish and the bugs and the river. I spent more time rummaging in my fly box, changing flies, lengthening leaders, moving around to see if I could find just one stupid trout, than I did casting. If there were other anglers nearby (and on the Willowemoc in May there are almost always other anglers nearby) I spied on them, hoping they were as frustrated and unsuccessful as I was. Mostly they were.

Between seasons I scoured my fly-tying books. I found new sulphur patterns and tied 'em all. I invented a few variations of my own, too, and the following May I showed them all to those Willowemoc trout. Once in a while I caught a couple of fish, and I thought, Aha. But then would come the refusals, and I realized I had not found any magic fly. Mostly the trout greeted them all with a sneer.

My only consolation during those several seasons of aggravation was the fact that nobody else seemed to have any better luck with the sulphur hatch than I did.

When I figured it out, it was by slow uncertain increments, not in one great burst of insight. First, I noticed that the riseforms in the early stages of the hatch did not break the surface. I guessed that they were eating emergers just under the surface. A little experimentation (well, a lot) led me to discover that a size 18 pheasant-tail flashback nymph dangled on six inches of 6X tippet from the bend of an unobtrusive dry fly would take some of those early fish. Casting down and across and twitching the nymph as it drifted into a feeding trout's sight windows would take more of them.

Their riseforms changed in subtle ways when they switched from subsurface nymphs to half-hatched emergers drifting in the film. Then I clipped off the nymph rig and tied on an emerger pattern similar to a fly that a guide showed me one day on Nelson's spring creek in Montana. This mongrel had a short, brown marabou shuck, a bi-colored body (brown for the abdomen, sulphur yellow for the thorax) with sparse thorax-tied ginger hackle, and a stubby gray cul-de-canard wing. This fly drifted low, half-sunk in the film. It would usually take some fish during the transition, and it was the nearest thing I found to a Magic Fly. In fact, even when their riseforms indicated that the fish had begun eating off the surface, my brown-and-yellow emerger would continue to catch an occasional trout, whereas no dun imitation I could find would elicit anything more than a half-hearted follow.

But, as the hatch progressed, the trout would begin to snub even my magic bi-colored emerger. Mayflies would continue to blanket the water, and the fish would continue to eat, and nothing in my fly box would entice them . . . and my frustration would return.

Then one evening—why hadn't I noticed this years ago?—I saw a dun pop to the surface and instantly take flight. As I watched, I observed that this happened consistently, and I thought: These bugs didn't spend enough time on the water to get eaten.

In a flash of inspiration, I tore my gaze away from the water's surface and looked up into the twilight sky. First I saw the swallows and martins and waxwings, a frantic chaos of birds darting and swooping over the river. Then I saw the clouds of insects. Swarms of swirling bugs. Spinners . . . and, yes, they were falling onto the water.

About then it dawned on me that these fish weren't even trying to eat the jittery newly-hatched duns. They were gobbling the vulnerable spinners. When they first lit, exhausted, on the water, the spinners' wings were still upright, and in the fading early-evening light they looked like duns. But when I looked closer, I could see that the spinners' wings were glassier, their tails longer, and their bodies rustier than the duns. And then I saw that amid those with upright wings, the water's surface was littered with spent-winged spinners.

The spinners were falling while the duns were hatching, and once the spinners started to hit the water, that's all the fish wanted.

Aha.

I got a lot of satisfaction from figuring all this out. I loved knowing what I was doing, approaching this lovely hatch with confidence, and catching trout on a fairly regular basis.

I'd worked hard for this understanding. It felt valuable and important to me. When I shared my Willowemoc pools with other anglers during the sulphur hatch, it was hard not to notice that I was catching more trout than most of them were. I was aware of the fact that sometimes other fishermen stopped to watch me hook and land a trout. I heard them muttering to each other, and I imagined they were saying: "That man must be one helluva good angler."

I confess I liked it, that feeling of superiority. I'm not proud of it, but there it is.

★ ★ ★

Now, as this guy on the Willowemoc was asking me to give away my hard-earned secrets, I remembered a July evening a few years earlier at the notorious Y Pool on the Swift River. Big trout were cruising the deadwater under the spillway, humping their heads and shoulders, eating . . . something. Midges, I thought, but I tried a dozen different patterns—various pupae, emergers, and adults—without a single take.

Meanwhile, the fisherman directly across from me kept catching them. Finally, I couldn't stand it. When he hooked, landed, and released yet another fat rainbow, I said, "Nice fish. What'd he eat?"

"Cigarette fly," he said.

Right, I thought. *Thanks a lot. Cigarette fly. Sure.*

"Never mind," I muttered.

"No, really," he said. "Dumb name for a fly, but that's what they call it. Here." He cast across the deadwater. His fly landed at my feet. "Cut it off and try it," he said. "I got plenty."

"Hey, thanks," I said.

I tried it. It worked. And I thought: Not only is that guy a good angler; he's also a good man.

The fragment of a poem by Edgar Guest called "Gone Fishin'" ran around in my head. My father had framed the poem and hung it on my bedroom wall when I was a kid. Back then, decades ago, I'd memorized all three or four verses, but now I remembered only the first:

A feller isn't thinkin' mean
Out fishin';
His thoughts are mostly good an' clean
Out fishin';
He doesn't knock his fellow man
Or harbor any grudges then;
A feller's at his finest, when
Out fishin'.

I knew what my father would do if somebody asked him for advice. Dad never thought mean when he was out fishin'.

I opened my flybox and plucked out a couple of rusty spinners. "They're eating spinners," I said to the man on the Willowemoc. I dropped the flies into his hand. "Take a couple of these, too," I said, adding a few of my magic bi-colored emergers. "For next time, early in the hatch."

"Hey, thanks, man." He gave me a big grin. "Appreciate it."

A few minutes later his rod arced, and when he laughed into the gathering darkness, I found myself smiling.

23

Moon Down

For most of my adult life I was a nine-to-fiver with family and other obligations, and the best time to go fishing was whenever I could—weekends and vacations, mostly. I didn't have the luxury of timing a trip to hit a hatch or waiting for promising weather conditions.

Lately, I've arrived at a time in my life when I can, at least theoretically, go whenever the spirit moves me. It's been interesting to observe that sometimes I am moved, and sometimes I'm not. I've tried to keep track of the comings and goings of my fishing urges, and this is what I've found out about myself:

The urge strikes quite regularly at dawn and dusk, particularly in the summertime.

It's especially strong on what my dad used to call "soft days"—cloudy, windless, warm, and misty.

On the margins of the season—winter, early spring, autumn—I want to go fishing around noon on warm sunny days when the air and water are most comfortable for man and fish.

When the mayflies are hatching, all bets are off. I want to go regardless of any other factors.

My angling urges seem, more or less, to coincide with the times when fish are most active and my chances of catching them are best. After a lifetime of going whenever I could get away, maybe my subconscious has internalized the variables associated with good and bad fishing. I've tried to pay attention to myself, and I'm convinced that my urges are instinctive, almost physical, not the product of rational analysis. I do not think: "I will catch a lot of fish if I go now." I go when that certain feeling comes over me. More often than not I have decent fishing. Sometimes I get skunked. My urges are not infallible.

On the other hand, I always have a good time.

★ ★ ★

I was reminded of this last June when I was in Arkansas and John Gulley offered to take a few of us night fishing on the Norfork tailwater.

I hesitated, biting back the impulse to say: *No, thanks. I don't feel like it. I'd rather sleep.*

Gulley cocked his head at me. "The gates are all closed. Low water and heavy cloud cover. A dead-dark night. Perfect conditions. We got some giant fish in this river. They'll come out to play tonight."

I couldn't turn that down. It reminded me that an optimistic prediction from a local expert was another variable that sparked my fishing urges.

★ ★ ★

I waded behind John in water halfway to my knees. The Norfork currents gurgled quietly in the darkness. A pair of barred owls called back and forth. From downstream came the muffled voices of our companions, T. L. and Tom.

After a while, John steered me out into the river until I was knee-deep in a soft current. "There's a sweet run out there in front of you," he said. "Plenty of room for a backcast. Throw it upstream at an angle, swing it down on a tight line, twitch it in. The bite will be soft. Just tighten on him. I'll be upstream, if you need me. Keep your headlamp off the water. When you catch one, face the shore if you need to turn it on to unhook him. Got it?"

"Got it," I said. I liked the fact that he said "when" instead of "if."

Then John was gone, and I was alone in the darkness. It took me a while to learn to cast without eyes, to feel the length of line in the air, to know when it had straightened behind me, and to sense when to pick up the retrieve for a new cast.

I kept peering around, trying to see. But I could see nothing. When I gave up trying, I found the rhythm of it, and everything worked better.

Casting blindly into the dark was pleasant and mind-cleansing, but pretty soon I began doubt that I'd ever get a strike. I would cast all night into water that I couldn't see, the same water for hours and hours, and eventually the sun would rise and we'd go home and go to bed.

In the dark, without a watch, with no stars or moon, it's impossible to gauge the passage of time. It felt as if I'd been there for hours, standing in the same place, casting repeatedly. But I'd probably been fishing for about half an hour when I felt a nip and a tug and then a strong pull, and then somewhere in front of me a fish sloshed.

I steered it in, turned to face the shore, and flicked on my headlamp. It was a nice brown trout, 18 or 19 inches long. Not one of Gulley's hogs. But a very satisfactory fish, and a different kind of fun in the dark.

It went like that for a while—now and then one of us would hook a trout. It wasn't fast, but it kept me tense and alert for the soft tug and gentle bump in the night out there at the invisible end of my line.

Then Tom and T. L. hooked up at the same time and, before they landed their fish, John had one on, and then my rod tip twitched and dipped, and four hooked fish were sloshing in the darkness.

And then we kept hooking fish. Somebody always had one on. Our voices, trying to sound cool but betraying excitement and awe, and the splashing and surging of fighting fish, echoed in the moist night air.

It's hard to say how long it lasted. At least an hour. Maybe two hours. I know that I landed nine trout, more or less one right after the other, interspersed with some unproductive casts and several missed strikes and a few brief hookups. The same thing was happening to the other three guys.

And then it petered out and stopped, and we went back to a lot of casting and an occasional hookup until the sky brightened and it ended entirely.

John built a fire and produced a coffee pot.

"Is it always like this?" I said.

"When we got competent anglers," he said, "we catch fish. Oftentimes an 8- or 10-pounder or two. As long as the water's down and there's no moon."

"I meant," I said, "that flurry we had, when everyone kept hooking up. It was like the river suddenly exploded."

"Often happens that way."

"That," Tom said, "was our Solunar period."

"You're joking, right?" I said. "That Solunar stuff. Mysticism. Astrology for anglers."

He shrugged. "There are those who swear by it."

"Period or no period," said Gulley, "we wouldn't've had any fishing whatsoever without that cloud cover. Moonlight on the water is the kiss of death. A bright night, it's not worth fishing. Doesn't matter how the sun and moon are lined up."

"I bet that flurry was a Solunar period," said Tom.

"Anybody happen to notice what time it happened?" I said. They all shook their heads.

"I guess we'll never know, then," said Tom.

"You boys want to go again tonight?" said John.

We definitely did.

★ ★ ★

Back in the 1930s, John Alden Knight observed that fish didn't feed consistently all the time, that they seemed to become active at certain times of day and night. He theorized that high-activity periods such as we had that night on the Norfork could be predicted.

Knight noted the central importance of tides to saltwater fishing and wondered if there was a similar variable to account for activity peaks in freshwater fishing.

If so, you'd know when to go fishing and when not to bother.

Knight studied 33 variables and concluded that the key was the position of the moon. When the moon was directly overhead or directly "underfoot," exerting maximum gravitational force, fish became active. These times, which might last as long as 3½ hours, Knight called "major periods." Halfway between the major periods were "minor periods" of ¾ to 1½ hours. Two major and two minor periods every day, for a total of ten prime hours of fishing.

His 1936 book, *Moon Up Moon Down*, explained the theory. Field & Stream has been publishing the monthly Solunar tables ever since.

Knight cautioned that weather and season and other conditional variables—an approaching cold front, for example, or moonlight shining on the water—affected fish behavior. But everything being relative, the Solunar tables, he claimed, predicted the best times to go fishing.

★ ★ ★

When I got back to my room that morning, I looked up the current month's Solunar tables. That night, we'd have a minor period at 10:30, followed by a major period at 3:50 AM. I'd wear my watch and give the Solunar theory a scientific test.

I had my gear ready to go at sundown. I felt the urge coming upon me.

And then it occurred to me that, if the pull of the moon influenced fish, maybe it also affected people. Maybe the Solunar tables had been predicting the comings and goings of my own fishing urges all this time.

That night, there were no clouds. The full moon shone on the water like daylight, and John called it off.

So much for science.

24

Dobbers and Trailers

Over half a century ago in his classic *Trout*, Ray Bergman wrote of fishing nymphs upstream on a dead drift: "In my estimation, this is the most effective way to use nymphs, but unfortunately it is also the most difficult method to learn."

Nymph fishing was less popular in the 1930's than it is today, but Bergman made no claim to having invented or refined the upstream natural drift technique. Nor did he claim credit for suggesting what, at least in hindsight, seems like the obvious, common-sense remedy for the difficulty of this method, which is determining when a trout has eaten the nymph.

"In the beginning," he wrote, "it may be advisable to use a dry fly on the leader as an indicator. In attaching this dobber or float, tie it on as short a tippet as you can manage and attach it to the leader from four to six feet above the nymph. A fly with good floating qualities is necessary, say a heavily tied palmer hackle of a color most visible to you. The purpose of this dry fly is to give you something to watch for indications of a strike.

Sometimes it will disappear quickly, at other times it will simply stop floating with the current, and often it will simply twitch slightly without going under the surface. All these signs signify a strike, and you must react quickly by striking back or you will miss the fish."

Oddly, Bergman did not mention the possibility that a trout might decide to eat the "dobber" instead of the nymph, but, of course, that would happen occasionally no matter how outlandish the indicator fly was.

In deep water, where the trout are hugging the bottom, Ray Bergman's rig does the job in a low-tech, all-natural way. Modern strike indicators made of cork, foam, impregnated yarn, or other unsinkable and highly visible materials, however, work much better. "Heavily-tied palmer hackle" dobbers lack the buoyancy to drift weighted nymphs without sinking, nor do they remain afloat for long in heavy, broken currents.

Another problem with Bergman's rig is that the dropper arrangement, the length of tippet between the indicator and the nymph, and the air resistance of the indicator fly all conspire to plague the fisherman with leader tangles. You have to cast it with a lazy, open loop—a method that does not allow you to false-cast the water out of your indicator fly.

If they don't offend your aesthetic sensibilities, synthetic strike indicators are the practical answer for upstream deep nymphing in heavy currents. But, with some refinements, Bergman's dobber-and-nymph rig will outfish foam or yarn better than two-to-one (a figure I just made up, which sounds about right) in slow-moving, shallow, clear water—especially when the trout are feeding at or near the surface.

It's no secret that even when mayfly duns and adult caddis-flies and midges are drifting on top, trout still target emerging nymphs and pupae. Often when they're maddeningly selective to dry-fly pattern they will eat almost any reasonable facsimile of the subsurface insect. I have found this to be especially true during blue-wing olive and sulphur hatches. The swirls and dimples of feeding trout pockmark the water, but no matter how precise my imitation, long and fine my tippet, accurate my cast, and natural my drift, my dry fly gets few takers. On the other hand, the fish happily gobble a pheasant-tail nymph. I have run into similar selectivity when caddisflies and midges are on the water. Soft-hackle wet flies and midge pupa imitations, drifted a few inches beneath the surface, consistently take trout that spurn the most true-to-life floating imitations.

The attentive and experienced angler can dead-drift subsurface flies upstream to visibly-feeding fish and do a fair job of guessing when his imitation has been taken, although there is always a lot of hit and miss. If a trout swirls or boils somewhere near where you think your nymph is, lift your rod. Sometimes you'll find a fish on the end of your line.

In this situation, a strike indicator improves your odds to nearly 100% (another fabricated statistic), which ain't bad. Any twitch or hesitation in the indicator means a trout has eaten your fly, and because you know your nymph is suspended beneath the indicator, you can usually tell which boil or swirl means business even before the indicator moves. The problem with the neon-colored synthetic indicator, even aside from the fact that it looks like a glob of trash floating on a pretty stream, is that in clear, slow-moving water it scares trout. Many times I've seen a trout approach my drifting nymph, spot the pink or chartreuse strike indicator, and dart away.

The trick is to choose for your "dobber" a close imitation of the floating fly that's actually on the water and that the trout might be eating. It should be visible, but not garish. On slow, smooth water all you need is something that you can see. Even a tiny, drab floater offers a visible silhouette, and a spot of color improves it. During those frustrating sulphur and blue-wing olive hatches, for example, I use a low-riding parachute imitation of the natural dun. Once in a while a trout actually eats it, but mainly it allows me to locate my nymph and detect strikes without frightening them. A parachute with a white post makes a pretty good imitation of an emerger or cripple. But I catch about 75% (beware of all angling numbers) of my fish on the unweighted pheasant-tail nymph (which closely imitates both the sulphur and the various blue-wing olive nymphs) that I trail behind it.

I use the same rig when fish are feeding at or just beneath the surface and I can't tell which, or what, it is they're eating. Often the water is littered with a smorgasbord of cripples, duns, spinners, terrestrials, and half-emerged nymphs. A dobber with a trailer at least doubles my chances of figuring it out, and it's easy enough to experiment with a variety of likely trailer flies until the fish submit their report.

Here are some other situations where trailing a subsurface fly behind a dry-fly dobber solves tricky problems:

—On my eastern ponds and, indeed, on waters both still and moving everywhere, trout often gluttonize on emerging midges.

They tend to select the pupae that hang suspended in, or just beneath, the surface membrane. Your imitation is impossible to see. But you can locate it well enough to detect a strike if you trail it behind a Griffith's Gnat or other midge adult imitation.

—Although stillwater "gulpers" (for which Hebgen Lake is justifiably famous) usually eat high-riding *Callibaetis* duns, I have sometimes found them fussy. Dangling a *Callibaetis* nymph (a pheasant-tail is close enough) under my parachute Adams has convinced me that even these surface-feeders gulp nymphs whenever they encounter them.

—At the early stages of any mayfly hatch, when duns are just beginning to pop onto the surface, it's helpful to assume that the trout are still focusing on nymphs and emergers. You can locate these fish by their swirls and bulges, but they ignore your dun imitation. Trail a nymph or emerger behind it at least until the trout tell you that they've switched to the high floaters.

—Trout can be especially selective when they're sipping spinners, but spinner imitations ride so low on the water that the angler simply cannot see it—especially during the low-light conditions when spinners tend to fall. Often trout "pod up" to eat rafts of spinners, so that figuring out which rise came to your fly is mere guesswork. I routinely use a parachute version of the insect with a visible post for a dobber and trail a hackle-tip or clumped-hackle-wing spinner behind it. The parachute isn't a bad spinner imitation—but the trout generally favor the more realistic trailer.

—Trout love ants and often select them over any of the other odds and ends they find drifting on the water. An ant makes a great "searching" pattern, too, but a realistic ant imitation, except in giant sizes, is typically impossible for the angler to see on the water. I trail ant flies, both floating and damp, behind a beetle or hopper or even a Royal Wulff (which trout eat more often than you'd expect) and miss few strikes.

—During any blanket hatch, when insects cover the water and every fish in the river is up gorging on them, locating your good imitation among all the naturals can be next to impossible. Trail a precise imitation behind a dobber that's a couple sizes bigger than the naturals, or that has a white wing or some other feature that allows you to distinguish it from the others so you can follow its drift. You won't be able to identify your trailing fly, but at least you'll know where it is, and when your dobber darts under the water, you'll know a trout has taken it.

—When trout appear to be eating adult caddisflies—but not your precise imitation—they might be feeding selectively on either emerging pupae or drowned adults. Dangling a pupa imitation or a soft-hackle wet fly under your floater is a good way to find out.

—In the absence of specific surface activity, the "hopper-dropper" has become the standard go-to searching rig among Western drift-boat guides (and it works equally well on eastern rivers). Drop a Copper John, hare's ear, or PT nymph off a high-floating grasshopper imitation and throw it against the bank. A beetle or ant dropped off a hopper/dobber makes a lethal combination.

★ ★ ★

Until I learned how to rig it, I rarely used a dry fly for a strike indicator. I got too many tangles and broke off too many fish.

Tying the dropper tippet to the bend of the indicator fly's hook is how I see it most commonly done. This method is strong and secure and minimizes tangles. The problem with it is that even a minimally-weighted nymph tends to sink the rear half of the floater, which looks unnatural and minimizes its appeal to trout. Besides, anytime a fish takes the floater, the trailing system becomes tangled.

Henry's Fork super-guide Bob Lamm showed me a better way to rig a two-fly system that casts without tangling, drops the weight of the nymph under the hackled part of the indicator fly, and has no weak links. First he ties a dry fly to the end of the tippet as if it were the fly he intended to catch fish on. Then he knots a 12–24-inch length of tippet of one size smaller diameter directly to the eye of the indicator fly and ties the trailing fly to the other end. I have found that with this set-up I can false-cast the water out of my floating flies and throw tight loops and all the necessary types of cast as effectively as I can with a single fly.

Now, whenever I expect to find fish at or near the surface, I usually rig up with two flies from the beginning. I make my best guess when I tie on the dobber, and I change the trailer as many times as I need to. The dobber-with-trailer setup gives me many advantages—and presents no handicaps that I've yet discovered.

25

Animal Wrongs

Until eight years ago, I didn't pay much attention to the animal-rights movement. I had a general understanding of what they believed (they thought the Bill of Rights applied to spiders and catfish and porcupines the same as to people), and I'd read about some of the stunts they'd pulled to promote their beliefs (mostly silly). I knew there were a few certifiably dangerous fanatics among them—people who burned down medical laboratories and threatened to murder researchers who used animals for testing and experimentation—but for the most part, they seemed to be harmless get-a-lifers.

In December of 1996, though, the animal-rights folks struck close to my home, and I decided I better take them seriously. PETA (People for the Ethical Treatment of Animals), the largest, best-funded, and most media-savvy of the myriad animal organizations, sent a letter to Peg Campbell, the head ranger at the Walden Pond State Reservation in Massachusetts, with copies to all the Boston and local newspapers, who dutifully reprinted it under headlines such as "Animal Activists Angle for Fishing Ban at Walden Pond" (the *Boston Herald*).

The letter was signed by Davey Shepherd, PETA Save Our Schools [get it? schools?] Campaign Coordinator. It said:

Dear Ms. Campbell:

On behalf of PETA's more than 15,000 members in Massachusetts, we would like to request that you ban fishing at Walden Pond.

As you know, fish have a neurochemical system like ours, the brain capacity to experience fear and pain, and sensitive nerve endings in their lips and mouths, and they begin to slowly die of suffocation the moment they are pulled out of water.

Fish have individual personalities, too. They talk to each other, form bonds, and sometimes grieve when their companions die. They communicate with one another through a range of low-frequency sounds (audible to humans only with special instruments), expressing courtship, alarm, or submission. Fish also enjoy companionship and develop special relationships with each other. And since they enjoy tactile stimulation, they often gently rub against each other.

We feel sure Henry David Thoreau would have wanted Walden Pond to be designated a sanctuary for all wildlife. He wrote more than 100 years ago, ". . . I cannot fish without falling a little in self-respect." Ending fishing at Walden Pond would be a wonderful tribute to the great humanitarian and his love for animals.

PETA has produced and would be happy to provide you with "No Fishing" signs free of charge to help institute the ban.

Please feel free to call me at 757-622-7382, extension 612, if you have any questions, and please let us know what you plan to do. Thank you for your time and consideration.

I'd fished for trout and smallmouth bass at Walden Pond since I was a kid. I'd lived in Concord, Thoreau's hometown. I'd studied his books about Walden, the Concord and Merrimack rivers, the Maine woods, and Cape Cod, and I knew that Davey Shepherd had taken Thoreau's fishing quotation way of out context.

Shepherd's anthropomorphic images of fish grieving and courting and enjoying "special relationships with each other" should have made me laugh.

But this was my Walden Pond he was targeting. It wasn't funny.

I called Davey's extension at PETA. He seemed to be a humorless, mild-mannered, intelligent man. He had an unmistakably British accent. It was unclear whether he'd read Thoreau. He asked me if I wanted some free No Fishing signs.

Davey referred me to Tracy Reiman, PETA's "national anti-fishing coordinator." She used phrases like "aquatic agony" and told me how a famous London designer was creating a costume for their anti-fishing mascot, "Gill the Fish," who they planned to send out to disrupt bass tournaments. Ms. Reiman explained that PETA also intended to exploit the power of the Internet to promote their agenda. "Ultimately," she told me, "what we want is for people not to fish."

Peg Campbell, the recipient of the PETA letter, just shrugged and smiled. She couldn't ban fishing at Walden if she wanted to—which she didn't—because to do so would violate the terms of the Reservation's deeds. PETA, she said, knew that. They really didn't expect anything to happen. It was all about publicity. She advised me not to worry about it.

But I *was* worried. Walden Pond really wasn't the point. There were millions of people who didn't know any better, well-meaning, non-fishing, soft-hearted, animal-loving folks whose common sense I didn't trust. They might fall for this non-sense. PETA, I knew, was deadly serious. They wouldn't give up.

They had my attention.

Shortly after the Walden letter, PETA took aim at catch-and-release angling, which they equated to "torture disguised as sport." Their arguments rested on the assumption that fish experienced pain and fear the way humans do. This seemed silly and far-fetched and self-serving, which probably accounted for the fact that their crusade against fishing wasn't gathering any momentum . . . until some Scottish scientists conducted experiments that, they claimed, proved that fish did, indeed, feel pain.

The researchers discovered that fish had nerve endings called "polymordal nociceptors" in their heads and mouths, just like people. Moreover, injecting bee venom into the nociceptors of rainbow trout produced "anomalous behaviours" that the researchers described as "strikingly similar to the kind . . . seen in stressed higher vertebrates."

In other words, fish felt pain . . . just like us.

The animal-rights propaganda machine proceeded to blitz the media with stories. Headlines such as "Fish DO Feel Pain, Scientists Say" appeared in newspapers and magazines, on television and the Internet. PETA chortled: We were right all along!

But wait . . .

Most of the stories didn't mention the fact that the scientists, following standard experimental procedure, had also injected a control group of trout with a mild saline solution. These control trout did not behave "anomalously," meaning that it was the bee venom—*not* the prick of the needle—that caused their "pain."

You don't have to be a scientist to realize that hooking a trout on a Size 6 woolly bugger is quite similar to pricking its lips with a hypodermic needle. If anything caused pain and fear in trout, the Scottish researchers proved that it was *not* jabbing something sharp into their mouths. Unless you soak your flies in bee venom, in other words, you won't cause anomalous behaviours.

As these things typically go, it's taken longer to debunk the fish-feel-pain hoax than it took PETA to promulgate it.

★ ★ ★

I'm keeping my eye on PETA and their anti-fishing crusade. Here's what they've been up to recently:

• They're trying to persuade the Boy Scouts to "demerit" its fishing merit badge.

• They've been publicizing the mercury and PCB contamination of fish—not to promote clean water for healthy fish, as you might expect, but rather as an anti-fishing argument.

• When the animated film "Finding Nemo" was nominated for an Oscar, PETA declared the movie a compelling manifesto against the barbaric practice of imprisoning fish in aquariums, the finny equivalent of "Bambi."

Oh, well.

I intend to keep my eye on the anti-fishing movement. Still, I think Peg Campbell was right. The PETA folks are a minuscule minority of true believers, earnest and committed, but not worth worrying about.

Peg's reply to Davey Shepherd's Walden letter put the whole issue into proper perspective:

Dear Davey:

Many thanks for casting us your letter regarding our chums, the fish. Many special interest groupers have tried to land us with the same line. At Walden Reservation we try to avoid being gaffed by such carping correspondence, so my response will be brief.

Our piranha budget is shrimpy and we cannot afford to spend any extra clams on such a project. Further, our mantapower situation is such that the park already shells out more than it makos.

You may think, this being Walden, that we are perched above the rest of the parks and that we don't get the blues or pout over the fate of our scaley friends. Believe me when I tell you that Walden is not a Gilled Lily. With less money, we are reely in a pickerel. Our roe boats are leaking; our head of grounds, Ray, is out with a shiner. The fact is, we are really skating on thin ice.

I won't string you along by casting about for other excuses. But many fishermen at Walden Pond are as attunaed to nature as you are. Oh sure, a few are basstards, but almost all of them have haddocked up to their littlenecks with half-baked ideas like yours. And while you flounder about trying to f-eel good about yourselves, most of these folks live in the reel world.

Frankly, Davey, I think your effort to try to a-bait sport fishing at Walden Pond is eel-advised. I see trout fishermen's hackles stiffening; indeed, it could easily spawn a whale of an uproar. I think their anger will truly shark you when you encounter it. This is something they love to do, and I assure you they won't give it up just for the halibut.

I hope my response wasn't too lure-id. My crabby disposition lately comes from dealing with so many suckers. Do drop me a line if you are planning to come to Walden. And take the Pike. It's faster unless you encounter a snag or a jam.

Sea you soon.

26

Mouse Ears
and Hendricksons

W hen I was a kid, our fishing season officially opened
when Charley Watkins called from Maine to announce that the ice had gone out at Sebago Lake.
Charley ran the ramshackle cabin-and-boat-rental up there, and
he knew that we Massachusetts boys were itching to go fishing
after a long New England winter.

"You fellas better git up here yestiddy," Charley would yell
into the phone. Charley yelled because he was stone deaf. "I got
Cabin Four waitin' for you."

"WE'LL BE THERE FRIDAY NIGHT," my father would
scream.

"You gotta speak up, Mr. Tapply," Charley would yell. "Must
be a bad connection. How's Friday night for you?"

Shortly after iceout on Sebago, the smelt began swarming in
the mouth of the Songo River. Landlocked salmon came from
all over the lake to feed on their favorite forage, and they would
strike Grey Ghosts and Warden's Worrys trolled on fly rods off
the stern of one of Charley's clunky old rowboats.

Charley Watkins' annual call came anywhere from the third week in April to early May. Eventually we noticed that no matter when he called, it was always just a day or two after the apple tree in our front yard—100 miles southeast of Sebago—burst into bloom. "Charley's gonna call tonight," my father would say. "He's got his eye on our apple tree."

We laughed about it. It was our superstition, one more case of connecting two unrelated events such as walking under a ladder and losing money on the stock market in a cause-effect way. It was, we thought, one of those random, inexplicable things, a coincidence, what logicians call a "*post hoc ergo propter hoc* fallacy," as if the blooming of an apple tree in suburban Boston actually caused the ice to go out of a lake in southern Maine.

But, of course, the connection between our apple tree and iceout on Sebago was not a coincidence. In nature, explanations are sometimes hard to find. But nothing is random.

★ ★ ★

As winter slides into springtime here in New England, we natives watch the trees that grow along the banks of our favorite trout streams. According to folklore—and by actual observation—when the year's new maple leaves reach the size of mouse ears, it's time to go fishing. That's when the Hendricksons—large, smoke-winged mayflies that trout find irresistible—will begin to hatch.

Observant fishermen in other regions have their own, equally dependable, Hendrickson predictors. On certain Catskill streams, for example, the first Hendrickson hatches coincide with the blooming of the dogwoods. On other rivers, anglers look for blossoms on the swamp violets or bloodroot plants.

Everywhere, in fact, the life cycles of riverside flora and aquatic insects and other creatures are intimately intertwined. On some Rocky Mountain streams, chokeberry blossoms signal the beginning of the salmonfly hatch. Golden stoneflies appear when the wild roses burst into bloom along the banks, and green drakes hatch when the marsh marigolds begin to flower. On other rivers, these links do not hold true. But the observant trout fisherman can discover different, equally reliable, signals.

In nature, all life cycles rotate according to the same, mysterious timetable. Migrating birds appear—and depart—in the identical sequence every year. Insects hatch, wildflowers bloom, ice forms and melts, animals emerge from hibernation and bring forth their young, trees turn color and drop their leaves, fish spawn. It's all ordered, predictable, and interconnected, and observing how it works is one of the pleasures of spending time out of doors, even if you're not a fisherman.

Early settlers gave the shadbush, a New England woodland shrub, its name. They noticed that along the coast the shadbush's white blossoms always opened just at the time when the American shad, an anadromous fish, first entered tidal rivers to spawn. Today's savvy shad anglers keep an eye on the shadbush. It occurs on different dates from year to year, but it always tells them when to go fishing.

Inland and at higher elevations, the blossoming of the shadbush coincides with the hatching of the white-winged caddisfly called, naturally, the "shad fly."

Of course, it's not coincidence, it's not folklore, and it's not mysterious. It's a science called *phenology*, from the Greek word *phaino*, meaning "to appear." Phenology is the study of how periodic events such as flowering, breeding and migration make their regular, interconnected, and sequential appearances, especially as they relate to climate and weather.

The more time I spend outdoors, the more phenological links I've noticed. When I spot the spring's first migrating redwing blackbird in the marsh across the street, for example, I know that the trout will be feeding on midges in my local trout ponds—and those two happy events always seem to coincide with my first woodchuck sighting in the pasture behind the barn.

When the iris blossoms open up in my backyard rock garden, I can count on finding smallmouth bass on their spawning beds in the big lake. The autumn's first blue-winged olive mayflies appear when the sumac turns scarlet along the riverbanks.

For the past several Octobers, I've noticed, the flight woodcock have flocked into the poplars on John's Knoll the very night that the last leaf drops off the old lightning-struck sugarbush beside the abandoned farmhouse at the crossroads.

Other irises, sumac patches, woodchucks, and maple trees don't have the same predictive qualities as these particular ones. These are my personal phenological connections, and they probably won't work for you. But discovering your own unique local patterns is the reward and pleasure of becoming an amateur phenologist anyway.

The unfolding sequences of natural events are more or less dependent on local weather patterns, climate, latitude, altitude, and even longitude. Spring moves north at about 100 miles a week—a nugget of ancient farmer's wisdom that the science of phenology bears out—and it comes earlier along the coast and at low elevations than it does inland and in the hills. Shad bushes blossom—and shad flies hatch—later in the Green Mountains of Vermont than they do along the Connecticut coast. It happens later some years than others, but barring catastrophic events such as flood and drought, the connections among these events are unchanging. They are linked in complex but logical ways to such measurable variables as the temperature of the earth and the sea, the phase of the moon, and the angle of the sun.

Old Charlie Watkins has been gone for many years. Now we have the Internet and the Weather Channel and hot-line phone recordings to tell us what's going on where, if you want to trust them, and we can still get local updates from friends with telephones. As for me, I'd rather watch the maple trees and shad bushes and redwing blackbirds and let my seasons unfold in their ancient, predictable, and comforting ways.

27

Bass Bugging Myths and Misconceptions

When I started going bass-bug fishing with my father, oh, close to fifty years ago, I was entranced by the utter simplicity of it. Anytime we could sneak away for a few hours, we brought a five- or six-weight trout rod and a small box of generic deerhair bugs, launched our canoe, and took turns paddling and casting along a shaded shoreline. We always caught some fish. Sometimes we caught many fish, and more than our share of big ones.

During the ensuing half century, a lot of so-called lore has been added to what Dad and I knew. Experts have written many books (I myself am guilty of a couple of them) and countless magazine articles. Scores of fancy new bass bugs have been designed. Specialized equipment has been invented.

If you didn't know better, you'd think bug fishing for bass was as complicated as dry-fly fishing for trout.

It's not. That's the Number One myth about bass-bug fishing. There are others:

Myth #2: You need heavy equipment to cast bass bugs.

Aside from raising and catching big bass on the surface, the most addictive aspect of bass-bug fishing is casting to all the interesting targets a shoreline offers. Bass lurk around structure and cover and won't move far to eat, so the angler needs to drop his bug into some tight spots. Bug fishing requires accurate casting, and a lot of it. Throwing an eight- and nine-weight line will quickly take the fun out of it.

A five- or six-weight outfit with a forward-tapered floating line will comfortably handle well-designed deerhair and foam bugs that big bass will eagerly devour.

Myth #3: A bug must imitate what bass are eating.

Bass are opportunistic feeders. They reflexively attack anything that appears lifelike. That's how they survive. Except in rare circumstances, bass cannot afford to be selective. The fish that just ate a fluttering moth will eagerly engulf a frog or a minnow or leech—or a twitching bass bug.

Those who sell bass bugs—and those who write books about them—want you to believe that you need dozens of imitative designs and patterns in a range of sizes and variations so that you can match every possible bass prey. If you don't have a broken-legged female leopard-frog bug with you, they suggest ominously, how can you expect to catch a bass that's feeding on broken-legged female leopard frogs?

Nonsense. Any bug that appears more or less alive on the water will trigger a strike from any bass that's looking for a meal. There is no evidence whatsoever that bass notice or care about "realistic" elements such as eyes, ears, gills, fins, arms, legs, fingers or toes on bugs, although there is considerable evidence that heavily-decorated bugs snag lots of anglers.

All that stuff just adds weight and air resistance to a bass bug and makes casting it a chore. A sprig of bucktail or marabou for a tail and a couple of rubberlegs whiskers up front gives a bug plenty of enticing wiggle. You can improve most commercial bass bugs by cutting off all the adornments.

Tie on any streamlined bug you that can cast comfortably with a mid-weight rod. Gurgler-style closed-cell foam bugs, Tap's deerhair poppers, and cork-bodied Sneaky Pete sliders all fill the bill. Make it slither and wiggle and go *glug, gurgle* and *ploop*, and it will catch every catchable bass that sees it.

Myth #4: Color matters.

Joe Brooks, whose 1947 book *Bass Bug Fishing* was, for the ensuing 50 years, the only one devoted exclusively to the subject, said: "East, North, South, West—it's all the same. Yellow is by far the best color." Other bass-bug fanatics swear by red-and-white. Every bug man, it seems, has his favorite color combination. That's what he ties on and casts with confidence, and lo and behold, that's what he catches all his fish on.

For subsurface flies, color no doubt matters. For floating bass bugs, color matters mainly to the angler. Most edible critters have pale bellies, so it's probably a good idea to tie on a bass bug with a white or yellow belly. Otherwise, when a bass swims over and squints up at that creature that just plopped onto the water and has begun twitching and wiggling, all it sees is that pale belly and the movement of a silhouette against the glare of the sky. I generally use white or yellow bugs . . . because I can see those colors best, not because the fish care.

Myth #5: Big bugs catch big bass.

No doubt. But so do small bugs and medium-sized bugs. I've caught many 4-pound-plus largemouths while casting little panfish poppers for bluegills. Of course, if you don't want to be bothered by small bass and panfish, you can discourage them with a big bug.

I've caught too many large bass to be convinced that a hungry bass of any size will pass up a well-twitched bug because it's not big enough but, even if it were true, I won't accept the trade-off. You need a heavyweight outfit to throw a big air-resistant bug, and pretty soon that becomes work, not fun.

Myth #6: Sulky bass can be seduced, fooled or angered into striking a bass bug.

Bass, like all wild creatures, are simple survival-tuned organisms. They behave instinctively. They don't think. They eat, they avoid predators, they seek comfort, and they reproduce. That's about it. When we use human emotions such as "angry" or "sulky" or "smart" or even "hungry," we're describing their behavior, not explaining it.

Bass eat what appears edible to them based on their previous experiences with eating, plus whatever instincts that come with their DNA. More often than not, they eat whatever is available and easy to catch. But sometimes they are not interested in eating. At those times, they will ignore vulnerable frogs and minnows and dragonflies, and they will surely ignore bass bugs, no matter how seductively you manipulate them.

Myth #7: You can't fish a bass bug too slowly.

This hoary myth persists as the conventional wisdom on how to retrieve bass bugs. Joe Brooks wrote: "The slower the retrieve, the better. . . . When [the bug] hits, let it stay where it is from one-half to almost a minute. Then give it a slight twitch with your rod tip, or even pop it. Let it stay motionless again for half a minute. Another twitch or pop."

Other experts recommend lighting a cigarette after casting a bug upon the water and smoking it down to the filter before giving the bug its first twitch. Others suggest eating a sandwich.

The same bass-bug experts inevitably follow up this advice by telling you to speed it up when the slow-motion retrieve doesn't work.

Nowadays, the real bass experts are the tournament pros whose income depends on catching fish. When they use surface lures, they generally cast 'em out and chug 'em back. If the relatively fast retrieve didn't work best, you can be sure they'd slow it down.

The fact is, sometimes one type of retrieve works better than others, for reasons only the bass know. Start with fairly fast retrieve, because you can cover more water that way. If you're not catching fish, slow it down and vary the cadence—twitch-pause-twitch, or, twitch-twitch-GLUG, pause, etc.—until the bass tell you what they like.

Myth #8: Don't give up on a good-looking spot.

Joe Brooks advised, "If you feel reasonably sure that a bass is in a certain spot, work it carefully. Throw your bug back time and again. I've often cast twenty times over a fish before he took."

The problem is, what looks good to you may not look good to the fish, and while you're investing the time it takes to make twenty casts over a barren piece of water, you're not fishing all the other water that may be more productive. Usually a hungry bass will hit your bug the first time he sees it, and if he's not hungry, there's not much you can do to change his mind.

However, bass rarely move far from their lairs to strike a bug, so be sure you cover all the bassy nooks and crannies. Hit every edge and pothole in a bed of lily pads. Twitch your bug past the tip, both sides, and the base of a fallen tree. Drop it against all sides of a boulder

After that, no matter how good that water looks, move on.

Myth #9: If you miss a strike, change flies and rest the fish before trying again.

If a bass follows your bug, or swirls behind it, or strikes at it and misses (which usually means you failed to hook him), you know he's interested. Don't let him off the hook. The bug you've got tied on, the one he came after, is the one that got his attention, and there's no reason to change it.

If you use a strip strike—as you should—leave your bug right there. Imagine that bass looking at it, trying to decide whether to try again. Give it a twitch. Make it glug. Start it moving. If he doesn't hit again, cast it back immediately to where he was originally lying.

However, if you felt any resistance when he hit the first time—if your pricked him, however lightly—forget about it. Bass don't grow into adults by ignoring such warning signs.

Myth #10: Bass bugs only work in low light.

Traditionally, bass-bug fishing is a dawn and dusk sport, and there's no doubt that those are the magic times on the water. Like most fish, bass don't like bright sunshine. But as long as the shallow-water temperatures are comfortable for them, you can catch bass on the surface any time of day. Concentrate on shady areas—the eastern shoreline in the morning, the western in the afternoon. Cast close to the bank, under overhanging bushes and trees, among reeds and lily pads, alongside boulders and drowned timber. Anyplace that provides a little shade is a potential bassy spot.

So the best time to go bass-bug fishing is . . . whenever you can. Simple as that.

28

Trout Eyes

The Bull Shoals dam was holding back water, and the White River was running low and slow and clear. Local trout maestro Wayne Reed had led John Barr and me through some woods to a classic nymph run where a long glassy pool narrowed and spilled through a cluster of boulders. Wayne put me at the head of the run, and I immediately began catching 10-to-14-inch rainbows, drifting a Pheasant Tail and a Copper John. For an hour or so my strike indicator kept twitching and dipping, and I was content.

Then, typically, I got itchy. Overhead, the Arkansas sun blazed high and bright in a cloudless sky, and upstream the slow flat pool began whispering "sight fishing" and "big fish" into my ear. Seductive, irresistible words.

Downstream, Wayne and John were laughing about something. I didn't want to hurt Wayne's feelings. He had, after all, brought us here and set me up on this hot hole. But I wanted to go hunting.

I reeled up, tugged at the visor of my cap, and began creeping along the edge of the pool.

It took a few minutes for my eyes to see and my brain to interpret what they were seeing, but pretty soon I began spotting trout in the shallow water along the inside bend of the pool. Rarely could I make out an entire fish. Mostly it was a slash of crimson, or the horizontal line of a trout's back, or the angle of a caudal fin, or the sideways dart of a head, or the wink of a white mouth, or a shadow on the rocky bottom.

But all I saw were small fish like I'd been catching on nymphs. I'd done that. The White was famous for its giant rainbows and browns. I wanted one of them.

I lost track of time as I focused hard and expectantly on every square foot of water, stalking like a heron one slow step at a time. When I finally paused, straightened my back, and glanced behind me, I saw that I'd moved several hundred yards. I'd reached the head of the pool, where the current pushed against a ledge, then curled and spilled between two large boulders.

I looked so hard it felt as if my eyes were going to pop out and, after a few minutes, I saw what I'd been hunting for. It was holding near the bottom in the cushion behind the nearest boulder: A large, greenish, ghostly shape. A trout. A big trout.

It was a tricky lie, the kind of sight-fishing challenge I love. The eddy behind the boulder wanted to drag my nymphs away before they sank to the trout's depth. I tried drifting them right along the edge of the current seam, hoping that the fish would dart out to grab one of them. But it didn't. I tried dropping them in the soft cushion right against the boulder with a lot of slack line, but some hidden current would suck them out into the quick water. I moved upstream, reached over the boulder with my rod, and let my nymphs slide down the other side. I added weight, changed flies. Nothing worked.

In the swirling eddy I sometimes lost sight of the fish, but when I shifted my position and got the angle of the sun just right, I spotted it again. All my efforts hadn't spooked it. It was holding right where I'd first seen it.

Maybe it just wasn't in an eating mood. Or maybe it was eating something that I wasn't imitating. Most likely I just wasn't getting my flies to it so that they looked natural and good to eat.

I reeled up and found a rock to sit on while I pondered the situation. Maybe I'd catch that fish and maybe I wouldn't. But I wasn't about to give up.

A few minutes later Wayne came along. "How's it going?"

"I'm having fun." I pointed with my rod tip. "There's a really big trout behind that boulder, and I can't catch it. You can't beat that for fun."

"Sight fishing, huh?"

I nodded. "Why don't you try for that fish."

"Nope. You found it, it's yours. Show me."

I got up and looked. The trout hadn't moved. I pointed. "Right there. See it?"

He shifted his position, tugged at the brim of his hat, adjusted his sunglasses. "Hm. No . . . Wait a minute. Okay. Yeah. I think I see what you see."

"Give it a try," I said. "I'd love to see you catch that trout."

★ ★ ★

Colorado guide Sandy Moore introduced me to the mesmerizing intensity of sight-fishing for trout one October morning almost twenty years ago. I haven't been the same since.

We were fishing the Frying Pan, hoping to tie into one of that river's famously piggy rainbows. I was high-sticking a mysis shrimp imitation through a deep slot and having no luck at it when Sandy came along. He watched me for a few minutes, then pointed and said, "Look. There you go. See it?"

I looked where he was pointing. "What?" I said. "I don't see anything."

He blew out a breath. "Right there. *Look*, man."

I shrugged. "I am looking. Sorry."

"Here." He took off his sunglasses and handed them to me. "Try these."

I took off my glasses and put his on. Suddenly I could distinguish every pebble on the stream bottom. "My glasses are polarized," I said. "What's with these?"

"Amber. Maximizes contrast."

"Awesome. I don't see any fish, though."

He sighed. "See that square boulder? Look two feet upstream and then one foot to the left. Just behind that rock with the white on it. Nice fish."

I looked hard, and suddenly I saw it. First I saw a crimson slash. Then the shape of its head materialized. Then the curve of its belly, then its wavering tail. A big fat rainbow.

"Now that I see it," I said to Sandy, "I don't understand how I couldn't see it before. It's obvious."

"You've got to find your trout eyes," he said. "Like bonefishing. It takes a day or two on the flats before what the guides call your bonefish eyes kick in. You need the glasses for vision. Polarized for the glare, amber for the contrast. And it's ideal if you have an overhead sun and you can climb a bank or a rock and look down into the water, and it helps if the surface is smooth. Even so, just being able to see isn't enough. Your brain has to recognize a trout, to understand what it is your eyes are seeing. You hardly ever see a whole fish. You look for a line or a color or a shadow or a movement. Some little anomaly that isn't a rock or a stick. After you've done that a few times, those little trout clues get filed away in your brain. Okay, so now that you see it, go catch that fish."

I adjusted my position and drifted my shrimp imitation onto the trout's nose. It was intense, knowing that my fly was approaching a large trout, anticipating the take, then feeling the let-down when the fly drifted past.

On the fourth or fifth cast I saw its head dart to the side. Instinctively, I lifted my rod and felt its weight and, a few minutes later, Sandy netted a 19-inch rainbow trout that was shaped like a watermelon.

I patted my chest and blew out a breath. "I thought I was gonna have a heart attack," I said. "I swear that was the most fun I've ever had catching a trout."

For my remaining days on the Frying Pan I cast only to specific fish that I had located. I spent a lot more time stalking along the banks looking into the water—hunting—than I did actually fishing. The harder I hunted, the more fish I began to see. Locating one of those anomalies that translated to "trout," estimating its size, watching the way it was feeding, planning a strategy, creeping into position, and then drifting a fly to an actual specific fish was an entirely new and utterly absorbing form of fishing.

Nothing, of course, is fool-proof. I've encountered many conditions and water types where sight fishing was impossible.

Sometimes my trout eyes and my brain don't communicate clearly. Sometimes I just can't see the trout I know are there.

And sometimes I see trout that aren't there.

★ ★ ★

Wayne peered into the water, then shook his head. "I can't catch that trout."

"Sure you can."

He grinned at me. "Well," he said, "if I'm seeing what you're seeing, that trout ain't a trout."

I looked again, and after a minute I saw it. My trout was a green-backed fish-shaped weed. It had a tail and a head and, I'd swear, gills and a dorsal fin. But, okay, it was a weed.

I shrugged. "Wishful thinking, I guess. No wonder I couldn't catch it."

"So," said Wayne, "how much time did you waste, trying to catch that big old weed?"

"Waste?" I said. "I didn't waste a second. I was having a wonderful time trying to catch that weed before you came along and spoiled it."

Epilogue:
A Birthday Trout

The last time my father and I fished together was on his 85th birthday. What had been, for most of my life, a fishing partnership that took us all over the northeast for everything that swam in fresh or salt water, had devolved to this: A ceremonial once-a-year September canoe float on a serpentine woodland trout stream a mile from his house.

We parked at the iron bridge, as we always did. I toted the canoe to the water, and Dad carried the paddles and fishing gear.

"You take the bow," I said. "I'm going to paddle."

"No," he said. "You fish."

"But it's your birthday."

"Right," he said. "So I get to do what I want. I want to paddle."

We'd been carrying on this same argument for about fifty years, and it always turned out the same.

A canoe paddle was still a wand in Dad's gnarly hands. He pushed us upstream against the stream's slow currents, pausing without comment when a deadfall or undercut bank or shaded hole came within casting range, telling me by how he aimed the canoe where he wanted me to drop my dry fly. After forty years together, no words needed.

I wasn't getting any strikes. Not surprising. Objectively, this wasn't much of a trout stream. They stocked it with brookies in the spring, but the stream ran low and warm in the summer, and we figured most of the trout either got caught or migrated down to the lake or died. Fishing was always pretty slow in September.

We loved the stream anyway, because it was inaccessible except by canoe from that one iron bridge, and because the fishing wasn't good enough to attract many other anglers. In all the years we'd floated it, we'd never seen another human being there.

We didn't really come here to catch fish. We came to this stream on my father's birthday . . . because we always did.

It rose in swamps in western Maine, meandered through miles of old hardwood forest, and eventually emptied into a New Hampshire lake. By the time Dad's birthday rolled around in September, the maples and oaks that canopied overhead were turning crimson and copper.

It was an awfully pretty stream in the fall, trout or no trout.

We'd been moving upstream for about an hour when we came to an uprooted pine that had fallen across the water. Back when my father was younger, he'd have insisted we drag over it or carry around it and keep going. In those days, he never wanted to turn around. But today when I suggested that this was as good a place as any to swap ends and head back, he nodded.

"My turn to paddle," I said.

"You keep fishin'," he said. "Catch something."

"These fish are too smart for me. Show me how."

"Oh, sure," he said. "Fish water you've already covered. Take your leavings."

Another one of our comfortable old arguments.

I had to help him out of the canoe. He staggered and held onto my arm as I helped him settle into the bow seat. He didn't grumble about his arthritic knees and hands, which meant they were really bothering him.

I steered us downstream, and he picked up the rod, tied on a little bucktail, and began flicking it against the banks. Watching my father from behind, the fluid, effortless way he cast, repeatedly dropping his fly about an inch from the bank, it was easy to remember him as a young man. He couldn't do a lot of things anymore. But he could still paddle and cast a fly.

The iron bridge was around the next bend when something boiled behind his fly.

I dug in with the paddle, and he cast again. Another swirl, and his rod bowed, and a few minutes later he was cradling a fat 14-inch male brook trout in his hand. Its spots were as scarlet as the streamside sumac, and its belly and pectoral fins glowed coppery like the oaks and maples over our heads.

It was maybe the biggest trout we'd ever caught here.

"Big stud wants to spawn," Dad said as he unhooked the fish and slid it back into the stream. "Let's wish him luck." He bit off the fly, reeled in, and took down the rod. "Good way to end it, huh?"

★ ★ ★

Raging arthritis, and then more serious miseries, kept my father out of canoes after that September afternoon. We celebrated the last six birthdays of his life in his living room, usually watching a ball game with the TV muted so we could talk fishing.

When we recalled our last birthday float, we agreed: It had indeed been a pretty good way to end it.